FLAVORS OF
MEXICO

**Authentic Recipes from
South of the Border**

**By Angeles de la Rosa and
C. Gandia de Fernández**

**Drawings by
Veronica di Rosa**

101 Productions

Recipes adapted from:
Cocina Mexicana, C. Gandia de Fernández,
 copyright © 1972 Editores Mexicanos Unidos, S.A.,
 Mexico, D.F.
Especialidades de la Cocina Mexicana, Angeles de la
 Rosa, copyright © 1975 Editores Mexicanos Unidos,
 S.A., Mexico, D.F.

Translated from the Spanish by Stephen Fredman

Flavors of Mexico copyright © 1978 101 Productions
Illustrations copyright © 1978 Veronica di Rosa
Cover copyright © 1988 Chevron Chemical Company
Cover design: Gary Hespenheide
Cover photography: Chuck Undersee

Published by 101 Productions and distributed by Ortho Information
Services, Box 5047, San Ramon, CA 94583

Library of Congress Catalog Card Number 88-71976
ISBN 0-89721-168-5

CONTENTS

Note Measurements in this book are not
straight conversions from U.S. measurements
to metric, but have been adapted into metric
for each individual recipe.

COOKING
MEXICAN STYLE

Mexico is, without a doubt, one of the richest countries in culinary art: The variety of dishes is infinite, so that we are certain no volume would ever suffice to display the numberless quantity of foods, all rich in flavor and refinement, which Mexican cooking sets forth. However, it is also difficult to allow that there is a Mexican who knows at most even one part of the great quantity of foods of his land.

We have intended to bring together in these pages the most interesting delicacies of Mexican cooking for your physical and spiritual benefit, since of course the aphorism "mens sana en corpore sano" is doubtless fulfilled by nothing better than a good meal.

We hope we have pleased you, friendly reader, and close this brief preamble with the wish: ¡gocen mucho! ("Enjoy yourselves!") Thus, our work will not have been in vain.

—Angeles de la Rosa

It is impossible to discuss Mexican cooking without marveling at the number of foods that tumbled from the cornucopia of Latin America when it was discovered by the Spanish. Many of these foods have become so assimilated into the cuisines of other countries that those cuisines are almost unimaginable without them—think of the Irish without potatoes, the Italians without tomatoes, the Hungarians, the Indians, the Orientals without chilies. Chocolate, pineapple, peanuts, vanilla, turkey, corn, pumpkins, sweet potatoes, squash—they have all become basic to the diet of the Western world.

Other foods that originated in Latin America are still somewhat unfamiliar or not always widely available, such as avocados, jícamas, chayotes, cilantro, papayas, *tomatillos* and plantains. Still other foods loved by the Mexicans are rarely, if ever, seen in the United States, such as zapotes, capulines, and many more.

Like these foods, the dishes that make up the Mexican cuisine are known to Americans living north of the border in wildly differing degrees of familiarity. Tacos and enchiladas have in the last few years become part of the diet of the United States, though often in versions that bear little resemblance to the Mexican dishes. But the vast majority of Mexican dishes have been only slightly heard of, and there is a fund of incomparable cooking to be explored by anyone interested in Mexican food.

Mexican food is basically Indian food, and in some ways it may strike the newcomer to it as very foreign, yet it is the closest thing we have in North America to an indigenous cuisine. Although the Indian cultures of Mexico were close to their primitive origins, they were also highly developed civilizations. The influence of the Spanish and other Europeans on Indian food has resulted in a vibrant cuisine that is at once primitive and sophisticated, simple and complex, ancient and alive.

ABOUT MEXICAN COOKING

Mexican cooking is as varied as the history and the landscape of the country, but two factors can be said to characterize cooking Mexican style. The first is simply that the best Mexican food is made with fresh tomatoes and fresh or dried chilies. Substitutions, however, are so often made that many people living in the United States have never had Mexican food made in the traditional way. Canned tomato purées have a canned taste as well as an acidy, over-strong tomato taste and a lack of any real texture. Although some recipes in this book call for canned chilies, they cannot substitute for fresh chilies in dishes in which their bright flavor and crunchy bite is important. Chili powder (a mixture of powdered chili, ground cumin, garlic and usually several other spices) is much used as an ingredient in Mexican food in the United States. Chili sauces are often made with powdered chili, a superior product, but one that must be mixed with flour to thicken the sauce, thus altering the taste of the sauce, while the texture in no way approximates the texture of a sauce made with dried chilies.

A second characteristic of Mexican cooking is that, because of the nature of the ingredients, organization and timing are very important in the preparation of a Mexican meal. Both tomatoes and chilies—two of the most common ingredients in Mexican cooking—require some preparation before the actual cooking of a dish can begin—and of course tortillas must be prepared also if you are making your own. Tomatoes are usually peeled and seeded, then chopped and puréed, though sometimes they are roasted for about 20 minutes before being used whole, or strained or puréed. Green chilies are usually seeded, deveined and cut up, but some of them must be roasted, then "sweated" for 15 or 20 minutes so that they can be peeled before using. Dried chilies are often toasted to make them pliable before they are seeded and deveined, then they are usually soaked in hot water for 30 minutes before being puréed, though some recipes with a milder or more subtle sauce will call for the chilies to be soaked overnight. Other ingredients, such as nuts and seeds, are often toasted or fried to bring out their flavor before they are added to a sauce; often whole spices must be ground, fresh herbs minced and unpowdered dried herbs crushed, all adding to the number of steps involved in the preparation of a dish.

Timing is very important in the preparation and serving of most tortilla dishes and some other dishes, such as Chiles Rellenos, as they must be put together at the last minute, with the other elements of the meal already prepared and just ready to serve. Tortilla dishes must be served as soon after assembly as possible, or they will become soggy with lard or oil and too tough in texture. Because of this, some dishes are especially open to abuse when not properly prepared, and they are particularly well suited to the home kitchen, where you can be sure of eating them within minutes of their creation.

INGREDIENTS

ACHIOTE The seed of the annatto tree, *achiote* is used extensively in Latin American cooking. In Mexico it is ground into a paste with a distinctive taste and dark red color, which is used to coat roasted foods or as an ingredient in sauces. *Achiote* is purchased as seeds or already ground into paste; if at all possible, try to buy the paste, as the seeds are very hard and very difficult to crush. If you are using the seeds, simmer them in a small amount of water for 10 minutes, then soak overnight. Crush in a mortar before grinding or blending with other ingredients.

ACITRÓN Candied cactus, used for its pale yellow color and chewy texture. Candied pineapple can be substituted.

AVOCADO LEAVES Not available in markets. They can be dried and stored for later use if you have access to a tree or a plant. Though the tastes are not very similar, a bay leaf can be used as a substitute.

BANANA LEAVES Used for wrapping foods in watertight packages; they provide very little taste or odor to food, and aluminum foil is an efficient substitute, though of course the leaves are much more appealing visually. Banana leaves are available in some Latin American markets; warm them in an oven set on low heat to make them flexible for wrapping.

CHAYOTE See page 125.

CHEESE Cheese is used a great deal in Mexican cooking, most often as a contrast in taste, texture and color to chilies and tomatoes. Some of the most common kinds of Mexican cheese are *queso añejo, queso blanco* and *queso fresco;* there are regional cheeses that are widely used, of course, as well. The only Mexican cheese called for in this book is *queso fresco,* a mild white cheese that should be available wherever Mexican foodstuffs are sold. It is usually packaged in small rounds. *Queso fresco* can be crumbled, shredded and sliced. It is used crumbled in dishes that require crumbled cheese essentially as a garnish. Natural cream cheese, made without emulsifiers and available in most health food stores and some ethnic markets, is listed as an alternate to *queso fresco* for crumbling; because it lacks emulsifiers it crumbles easily, and its flavor is far superior to commercial cream cheese.

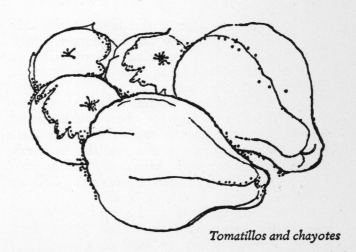

Tomatillos and chayotes

Queso fresco and Monterey Jack are often given as choices for recipes requiring shredded cheese (use the large holes of a grater for shredding); here the choice of cheese rests on taste and availability—Monterey Jack is more widely available and melts more easily, though you may prefer the saltier taste and whiter color of *queso fresco* if you can get it.

Recipes that require a shredded cheese that melts smoothly and easily call for Monterey Jack alone. You can also experiment with different kinds of mild white cheese, such as the Fontinas and mild white Cheddars.

Monterey Jack and natural cream cheese are usually listed as choices for cheese to be sliced thinly and placed on the top of a dish to melt slightly. Monterey Jack is also available in a very creamy form that melts beautifully and is very mild and fresh in taste; however, it is more difficult to slice than regular Monterey Jack.

Recipes calling for a hard grated cheese will specify dry Monterey Jack, a dark yellow aged cheese; Parmesan can be used as a substitute, though it is stronger in flavor.

CHILIES

Chilies vary tremendously in taste and appearance, not only from variety to variety but within the same type—*chiles poblanos*, for example, can range from small to large, and from fairly mild to *picante*. Green chilies are used fresh, while chilies that have ripened to red are usually dried. The many kinds of chilies can be confusing to a cook not familiar with them, and it is true that both fresh and dried chilies usually require several steps of preparation, but they are far superior to any substitutes. Note: Caution must be used when cooking with chilies, both fresh and dried. Be careful not to rub your eyes or mouth while handling them, and be sure to wash your hands well with soap and water when you've finished.

FRESH CHILIES The three fresh chilies most often used in this book are *serranos, jalapeños* and *poblanos*. They are listed below in order of size, from the smallest to the largest, followed by one fresh chili used here with less frequency. A variety of other fresh chilies are available seasonally in many markets in the United States, including Anaheim and cayenne chilies. To add to the confusion, chilies in markets may be misnamed, or not identified by name, often being labelled only as "hot peppers." Experiment with different varieties if Mexican chilies are unavailable.

Chile Serrano The smallest of the fresh chilies used in this book, it is slim, narrow and firm, a medium green in color, and up to 2 inches (5 cm) long, though it can vary in size and appearance. Available canned in vinegar. Sharply *picante*. Substitute any hot fresh chili.

Chile Jalapeño Larger, wider and not as firm as the *serrano*, the *jalapeño* is also quite *picante*, but slightly more complex in flavor. Available canned in vinegar. Substitute any hot fresh chili.

Chile Poblano Usually 3 to 4 inches (8 to 10 cm) long, and a very dark green with a wide top; the skin is wavy and dimpled and the chili may be slightly bent in the center. Usually slightly *picante* but with a deep, mellowed flavor that really has no substitute for taste, although green bell peppers are often used in place of *poblanos* in stuffed chili recipes, and strips of canned unpeeled green chilies are used in other recipes in place of strips of *poblanos*. Almost always roasted and peeled before using.

Chile Güero A waxy yellow or yellow-green chili that is slightly larger than, but similar in shape to, the *jalapeño*. *Picante*. Substitute any hot fresh chili.

DRIED CHILIES The *chile ancho* is the most-used dried chili in this book. If you do not have access to Mexican markets you can order dried chilies from a mail-order source; they will keep almost indefinitely. All are *picante*.

Chile Ancho The *chile poblano*, ripened and dried. Dark brown with a reddish tinge.

Chile Mulato Very similar to the *ancho* in appearance, but darker in color. The *ancho* may be substituted for it.

Chile Pasilla The dried *chile chilaca*, very dark in color. More *picante* than the *ancho*.

Chile Cascabel A small round shiny chili.

Chile Chipotle A dried, smoked *jalapeño*. Widely available in cans.

Chile Pequín Very tiny; usually used in powdered form.

CHOCOLATE See page 152.

CHORIZO SAUSAGE Spanish *chorizos* are made of smoked meat and are usually firm and easily sliced; Mexican *chorizos* are fresh, soft and lumpy. They can be used interchangeably.

CILANTRO Fresh coriander, also known as Chinese parsley. One of the most distinctive tastes in the Mexican cuisine, fresh coriander tastes completely unlike dried coriander seeds. It may well be an acquired taste, so use it sparingly if you or your guests are unused to it. People who like it find its taste incomparably fresh and clean; minced or used as a garnish it adds much visually to food. Available in Chinese markets, as well as in Mexican markets.

CORN HUSKS See page 69.

CREAM Use fresh, non-sterilized heavy cream. In recipes calling for sour cream, use natural sour cream if you can find it; it is made without stabilizers and available in some health food stores and ethnic markets.

EPAZOTE An herb with a strong, distinctive taste. Like *cilantro*, it is probably an acquired taste. It is rarely available in markets though it does grow wild in the United States. It should be considered an optional ingredient in this book.

JÍCAMA A brown-skinned root vegetable with a sweet white flesh. Found in Mexican and Chinese markets.

LARD Lard is the traditional cooking fat for Mexican food; it is listed as the first choice in most recipes (some very delicate dishes are exceptions) because it gives the food a characteristic Mexican taste. It is truly essential in very few recipes, however, and corn or safflower oil can usually be substituted. Use lard made without stabilizers, if you can find it.

MASA HARINA See page 44.

NOPAL CACTUS The pads of the prickly pear, available fresh in some markets as well as canned (plain and in vinegar); when cut into small pieces they are called *nopalitos*. To cook, see page 33.

Cilantro and epazote

PILONCILLO Unrefined sugar molded into little flat-topped cones. Dark brown sugar can be substituted.

PLANTAINS Very similar to bananas in taste but firmer in texture. They should be black-skinned and soft. Firm bananas can be substituted.

PUMPKIN SEEDS Used untoasted and unsalted; available in Mexican markets as *pepitas*.

SEVILLE ORANGES The sour oranges used to make orange marmalade. If you cannot find them, add lemon juice to fresh orange juice to approximate the tart taste.

SQUASH BLOSSOMS See page 24.

TOMATES VERDES *(Tomatillos)* Husk tomatoes are usually the size of small plums, and are light green in color and very firm, with thin husks that are easily removed. Available fresh in Mexican markets; widely available canned. Husk tomatoes are known as *tomates verdes* in Mexico, but are marketed canned in the United States as *tomatillos*, and are referred to as *tomatillos* in this book. To prepare fresh *tomatillos* for sauces, simmer them in water to cover until tender, about 10 minutes.

TOMATOES Only fresh tomatoes are used in the recipes in this book; canned tomatoes can be used in equivalent amounts in most cases if good fresh tomatoes are unavailable, but fresh tomatoes are always preferable.

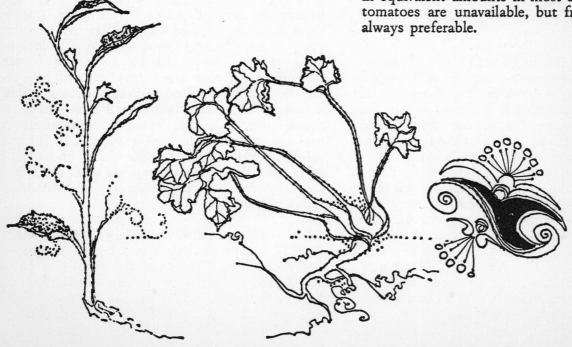

METHODS

COOKING MEATS AND CHICKEN FOR SHREDDING Place the meat, cut into chunks, or the chicken, cut into serving pieces, in a saucepan with salted water to cover. Bring to a boil, then reduce to a simmer. Cover partially, with the lid just askew to let the steam from the liquid escape, and simmer until tender, 45 minutes for chicken and pork, slightly longer for beef. Remove from heat, uncover, and let meat or chicken cool to lukewarm in the broth. Drain the meat or chicken in a colander or sieve, reserving the broth for the recipe you are using or for another dish (boil the broth until slightly reduced if you want it to be stronger). Skin and bone the chicken. Shred the chicken meat or the pork or beef with a fork into either fine or coarse pieces, as you like.

PEELING AND SEEDING TOMATOES If you are using tomatoes in quantity, plunge them, a few at a time, into a large pot of boiling water for 30 seconds, then remove with a slotted spoon and plunge into cold water. Cut out the hard stem-end section and slip off the peels. Cut the tomatoes in half and hold each upside down in the palm of your hand, squeezing slightly to remove the seeds. If you are only using 1 or 2 tomatoes, you may want to impale each on a fork and hold it over an open flame on the stove, turning until the skin blisters, then follow the above instructions.

PURÉEING TOMATOES AND CHILIES For a very smooth sauce, place the tomatoes or chilies (or both, as the recipe specifies) in a blender container and blend until smooth; add a very small amount of liquid to make a smooth sauce if necessary. For a sauce with more texture, purée the tomatoes and/or chilies through the coarse disc of a food mill.

ROASTING AND STRAINING TOMATOES Place the unpeeled tomatoes in a hot, heavy skillet over low heat and cook for 20 minutes or until tender, turning occasionally. Remove the hard stem-end section and purée the tomato with seeds and peel if you want a coarsely textured sauce, or purée in a food mill with a fine disc or force through a sieve if you want a smooth sauce.

ROASTING, PEELING, SEEDING AND DEVEINING GREEN CHILIES The *chiles poblanos* are usually roasted and peeled before using. Impale them on a long-handled fork and lay them on the open flame of a gas stove, turning occasionally until the skin is well charred and blistered all over (if you do not have a gas stove, you will have to put them under a broiler). Put the hot chilies inside a plastic bag, close tightly, and allow them to "sweat" for 15 or 20 minutes. Remove them and peel off skins under running water. Cut out the stem-end sections and cut the chilies open. Hold under running water to remove the seeds and veins. Drain on absorbent paper. Wash your hands with soap and water.

TOASTING, SEEDING AND DEVEINING DRIED CHILIES Place the chilies in a heated, ungreased heavy skillet and toast for a few seconds only, stirring and turning, until they are warmed through lightly. Slit open and remove the seeds and veins, reserving some of the seeds if the recipe you are using calls for them, or for future use, if you like. Wash your hands with soap and water.

TOASTING NUTS, LEAVES, SEEDS, GARLIC Nuts, seeds and garlic are often toasted in a heated, ungreased heavy skillet until just lightly browned; stir and watch them carefully so that they do not burn. Herbs and leaves are often heated lightly in the same fashion to bring out their flavor.

EQUIPMENT

BLENDER Called a *liquedore* in Mexico, the blender has taken much of the drudgery out of preparing Mexican food, replacing the grinding stone and the stone grinder (the *metate* and *mano*). You may need to add a small amount of liquid to some ingredients in order to keep the blades unclogged.

EARTHENWARE Some recipes suggest cooking in earthenware dishes. This is not necessary, but it is believed that the taste of some foods, such as beans, is superior when cooked in earthenware rather than metal. Earthenware casseroles and the *olla*, the deep, slightly narrow-necked pot used for beans and some beverages, can be used to both cook and serve, especially the decorative Mexican ones. Be sure that your earthenware is of good quality, as poorly glazed earthenware can have a dangerously high lead content. Care must also be taken in heating earthenware on top of the stove; always use a metal heat deflector under an earthenware container to prevent it from cracking. Never store food or beverages in the refrigerator in an earthenware container and then heat it on the stove, as the sudden temperature change will cause the container to crack.

FOOD MILL A food mill, especially one with a coarse disc, is preferable to a blender for use in some recipes, as the blender will purée sauce ingredients so smoothly that the desired rustic character of some sauces will be completely lost. Most recipes give the blender as a first choice for the sake of convenience; use your own judgement as to which you prefer for a given recipe.

MORTAR AND PESTLE A mortar is a great help in cooking Mexican food. Use it for grinding and crushing small amounts of foods such as whole spices and herbs. The classic Mexican mortar and pestle (*molcajete* and *tejolote*) are rough-textured and very efficient.

SKILLETS At least two large, heavy skillets, preferably of seasoned cast iron, are essential for use in the following recipes. A heavy griddle, also preferably of cast iron, can be used for toasting ingredients, and is a little more convenient than a skillet for cooking tortillas. The Mexican griddle used to cook tortillas is called a *comal*.

SPICE AND NUT GRINDERS A nut grinder is preferable to a blender for grinding all nuts except almonds, as a blender will make the ground nuts too oily. Use a mortar for small amounts of whole spices and herbs, or keep a peppermill to be used just for grinding spices. Note: It is helpful to crush cinnamon sticks with a rolling pin before grinding (place them between pieces of waxed paper to crush).

APPETIZERS

APPETIZERS *(Antojitos)*

The word used in Mexico for appetizers is *antojitos* (literally, "little whims"), and it commonly refers to snacks that can be eaten out of hand throughout the day. Many of the tortilla dishes that are thought of as main dishes in the United States are considered snack food in Mexico; these include tacos, *quesadillas,* burritos and other tortilla dishes without a sauce poured over. Many of these dishes can be adapted for use as before-dinner or party appetizers simply by making them with smaller tortillas, such as a 4-inch (10 cm) "cocktail" size (see Tortillas). The following dishes can be adapted in this way:

Quesadillas
Quesadillas Potosinas
Burritos
Burrita Norteña
Tacos
Tacos de Aguacate
Tacos de Frijoles con Chorizo
Panuchos de Picadillo
Taquitos de Rajas

Other dishes that can serve as appetizers:

Empanadas de Santa Rita (made small to
  become *empanaditas*)
Albóndigas
Albóndigas de Pescado
Camerones en Frio
Frijoles Refritos (with Tostaditas)

CEBICHE ESTILO ACAPULCO
Marinated Fish Acapulco Style

Cebiche (also spelled *seviche*) is one of the most elegant of all appetizers or first courses, especially in warm weather or before a heavy meal.

Serves 8 to 10
1 pound (500 g) red snapper, shrimp or scallops
Juice of 6 limes
8 ounces (250 g) tomatoes, peeled, seeded and
  chopped
4 *chiles serranos* in vinegar, drained and
  chopped
4 tablespoons (60 ml) olive oil
1 tablespoon (15 ml) white vinegar
1 tablespoon (15 ml) chopped cilantro or
  parsley
Salt and ground white pepper to taste
Thin slices white or red onion
Thin slices avocado

Cut the fish or scallops into bite-size cubes; leave shrimp whole unless very large. Place in a porcelain or glass bowl and pour the lime juice over. Refrigerate for 3 or 4 hours, stirring several times during this time period to make sure all the fish is well marinated. Add the tomato, chilies, oil, vinegar, cilantro or oregano and salt and pepper to taste and stir gently. For an appetizer, serve in a dish lined with romaine lettuce leaves and accompany with a bowl of food picks. For a first course, serve in cups or small shells. Garnish with slices of onion and avocado.

GUACAMOLE
Avocado Dish

Although it has been widely adopted in the United States as an appetizer, guacamole is much more versatile in Mexican cooking. It can be used as a vegetable side dish, a salad, a sauce, a garnish for or an ingredient in countless dishes, and as a dip with crisp-fried tortilla pieces or an appetizer spread on hot tortillas. The seasonings can be varied according to taste, the consistency can be smooth or coarse, and ingredients can include tomatoes and *tomatillos* (see the following recipes). Placing an avocado seed in the guacamole is believed to keep the sauce from darkening, but to assure a bright green guacamole, make the dish as close to serving time as possible. (If you must make the guacamole much ahead of time, cover it tightly with plastic wrap and do not add the salt until just before serving.)

Makes about 3 cups (750 ml)
3 avocados
2 *chiles serranos,* or
    powdered *chile pequín* to taste
1 small white onion, or
    2 garlic cloves
1 branch cilantro
1 tablespoon (15 ml) olive oil
Salt to taste
Freshly squeezed and strained lemon or
    lime juice to taste (optional)

Peel the avocados, remove the seeds (reserving 1 seed to place in the center of the guacamole, if you like), and place the avocados in a blender along with the chilies or powdered chili. Chop the onion coarsely and add it to the blender (if you are using garlic cloves, they can be added whole to the blender) along with the cilantro and the oil. Blend to a purée, then season to taste with salt and lemon or lime juice, if you wish. Alternately, mash the avocados with a wooden spoon. Finely mince the *chiles serranos* (if used), onion or garlic and cilantro and add to the mashed avocados. Stir in the oil and season to taste with salt and lemon or lime juice, if you like. Place in a decorative dish to serve.

GUACAMOLE CON TOMATE VERDE
Avocado Dish with Husk Tomatoes

A very green, mild guacamole.

Makes about 3 cups (750 ml)
1 pound (500 g) *tomatillos,* husked, or
  2 cups (500 ml) canned *tomatillos,* drained
1 *chile serrano,* seeded
1 small white onion, quartered
3 medium avocados
1 tablespoon (15 ml) olive oil
1 tablespoon (15 ml) chopped cilantro
Salt to taste

Put the *tomatillos,* chili and onion in a saucepan and add water to cover. Bring to a boil, reduce heat and simmer, covered, until the *tomatillos* are tender, about 10 minutes. Drain. (If you are using canned *tomatillos,* cook the chili and onion in water to cover until tender, then drain and add to the *tomatillos.*) Purée the vegetables in a blender or food mill. Peel the avocados and remove the seeds (reserving 1 seed to place in the guacamole, if you like), and either mince them finely or mash them with a fork. Add the *tomatillo* mixture to the avocados, then add the olive oil, cilantro and salt to taste. Mound the guacamole in a decorative dish to serve.

GUACAMOLE CON JITOMATE
Avocado Dish with Tomatoes

A coarsely textured, colorful guacamole.

Makes about 3 cups (750 ml)
3 medium avocados
1 pound (500 g) tomatoes, peeled, seeded and
  chopped
1 tablespoon (15 ml) chopped white onion
1 tablespoon (15 ml) chopped cilantro
1 tablespoon (15 ml) olive oil
Seeded and chopped *chile serrano* to taste
Salt to taste

Peel the avocados, remove the seeds (reserving 1 seed to place in the guacamole, if you like), and cut the avocados into small dice. Mix the diced avocado with the chopped tomatoes and add the remaining ingredients. Place in a decorative dish to serve.

QUESO RELLENO
Stuffed Cheese

A unique dish from Yucatán, reflecting the Dutch influence in the Caribbean.

Serves 8 to 10
1 4-pound (2 kg) Edam cheese
3 or 4 hard-cooked eggs
1 pound (500 g) ham, coarsely chopped
1 slice cabbage
1/2 onion, coarsely chopped
1 green bell pepper, seeded and coarsely chopped
1 medium tomato, peeled, seeded and coarsely chopped
1 cup (250 ml) water
10 pitted green or black olives, chopped
2 tablespoons (30 ml) raisins
1 tablespoon (15 ml) capers
Salt and freshly ground black pepper to taste

Cut a 1/2-inch (1 cm) "cap" slice from the top of the cheese, peel off the wax covering and reserve the slice of cheese. Hollow out the inside of the ball with a spoon (reserve this cheese for another use) leaving a 1/2-inch (1 cm) shell. Peel the wax covering from the cheese; set the cheese aside.

Peel the egg whites from the eggs, leaving the yolks whole. Set the yolks aside, then finely chop the whites and set aside. Place in a blender the ham, cabbage, onion, pepper and tomato and coarsely purée. Place the puréed mixture in a saucepan, add the water, and cook for 5 minutes over medium heat. Add the olives, raisins, capers and reserved chopped egg whites. Add salt and pepper to taste and cook and stir until the mixture is almost dry.

Place half of the meat filling in the hollowed-out cheese, then add the egg yolks in a layer and top with the remaining meat filling. Place the "cap" on top of the cheese and wrap the cheese tightly in a muslin cloth, tying it firmly closed with cotton string. Set in a bowl in a steamer to which water has been added, cover the steamer and cook for 15 minutes or until the shell is just softened. Remove the cheese from the steamer and unwrap it, placing it in a covered container to keep it warm, if necessary, before serving. To serve, discard the "cap" and place the cheese on a decorative plate with a serving spoon. Accompany with hot tortillas to be filled and folded like tacos.

TOSTADITAS DE CHILE ANCHO
Tortilla Triangles with *Chile Ancho* Sauce

The simplest Mexican appetizer of all is freshly fried tortilla triangles, kept warm in a basket lined with a cloth napkin and served with one or more *picante* sauces. They are also known as *totopos,* a name otherwise given to tortillas cut into small squares as a garnish. The chili sauce given here is quite *picante;* a list of other sauces for *tostaditas* is given at the end of this recipe.

Makes 48

Salsa de Chile Ancho
4 *chiles anchos,* toasted
1 garlic clove
2 tablespoons (30 ml) chopped onion
1 tablespoon (15 ml) white vinegar
Salt to taste
1/2 cup (125 ml) grated dry Monterey Jack
   or Parmesan cheese

Tostaditas
8 corn tortillas (stale tortillas may be used), cut
   into 6 triangles each
Melted lard or corn or safflower oil to 1/4 inch
   (6 mm)
Salt

To make the sauce, soak the chilies for 30 minutes in boiling water to cover (if you prefer a milder sauce, remove the seeds and veins from the chilies before soaking). Drain the chilies, reserving the soaking water, and place them in a blender along with the garlic, onion and vinegar. Purée the chilies, adding the reserved soaking water as necessary to make a coarse sauce. Add salt to taste. Just before serving, stir in the cheese.

To make the *tostaditas,* in a heavy skillet, heat the melted lard or oil to the smoking point. Add the triangles in small batches, turning them as they cook until they are crisp and golden. Drain on absorbent paper and sprinkle lightly with salt; serve warm with Salsa de Chile Ancho, one or more of the following sauces, or with Guacamole or Frijoles Refritos.

SAUCES FOR TOSTADITAS

Salsa de Jitomate
Salsa de Tomate Verde
Salsa de Chipotle y Aguacate
Chile Frito
Salsa de Chile y Cebolla

SOPES
Tortilla Appetizers

Simpler to serve and eat away from the table than filled tortillas, *sopes* are little molded tortilla "bowls" to be filled and served hot. They may be toasted ahead of time and fried just before serving. When shaped into little "canoes" they are called *chalupas*. To make *gorditas* ("little fat ones"), form the dough into thick little tortillas without shaping them into bowls, then toast, fry, sprinkle with grated cheese and heat under a broiler until the cheese begins to melt (also try spreading *gorditas* first with Frijoles Refritos).

Makes about 12
1 pound (500 g) fresh *masa*, or
   1-1/3 cups (325 ml) *masa harina* and
   1/2 to 3/4 cup (125 to 175 ml) water
A pinch of salt
3/4 cup (175 ml) grated dry Monterey Jack or
   Parmesan cheese
3 tablespoons (45 ml) lard or corn or safflower oil
1 tablespoon (15 ml) minced onion
1 garlic clove, minced
8 ounces (250 g) tomatoes, roasted
1 cup (250 ml) Frijoles Estilo Mexicano, mashed,
   or Frijoles Refritos
Salt to taste
Seeded and chopped *chile serrano* to taste
Melted lard or corn or safflower oil to
   1/4 inch (6 mm)
1/4 cup (75 ml) shredded Monterey Jack cheese

Mix the fresh *masa* with the salt and cheese. (If using *masa harina,* add water and stir quickly, then mix in salt and cheese.) Divide the dough into 12 equal parts and form into balls, then flatten into tortillas 1/4 inch (6 mm) thick. Lightly oil a griddle or a heavy skillet and place over medium heat. Toast each tortilla lightly on one side, then turn over and, while it is cooking, lift up the edges of each tortilla and pinch to form a bowl (or toast each tortilla for a few seconds, then remove it to a plate before shaping; return to the pan to toast a few seconds longer). Set the *sopes* aside and keep warm.

In a heavy skillet, heat the 3 tablespoons (45 ml) lard or oil and cook and stir the onion and garlic until translucent. Add the roasted tomatoes and cook and stir until slightly thickened, about 5 minutes. Add the mashed beans, season to taste with salt and chili and cook and stir until heated through; set aside and keep warm. In another heavy skillet, heat the lard or oil almost to the smoking point and fry the toasted *sopes* lightly, spooning the lard or oil into the *sopes* to fry the interiors as well. Remove the *sopes* from the skillet and drain them on absorbent paper. Quickly fill them with the bean-tomato mixture, top each with 1 teaspoon (5 ml) cheese, and place under a broiler until the cheese begins to melt; serve at once.

FILLINGS FOR SOPES

Sopes can be filled with chopped fried *chorizo* sausage, with almost any combination of sauces and shredded meat or chicken, or with meat fillings cooked in a sauce (see Fillings for Tacos for specific suggestions). In place of the grated cheese topping, top each *sope* with a spoonful of sour cream and a sprinkling of chopped cilantro, or top with chopped green pumpkin seeds; do not broil. Also, try *sopes* filled with grated cheese and chopped green chilies, melted under a broiler and served plain or topped with a spoonful of Salsa de Jitomate.

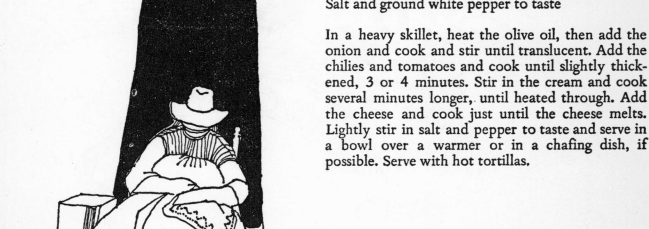

CHILE CON QUESO
Chilies with Cheese

A savory and satisfying hot appetizer to spread on hot tortillas.

Serves 6 to 8
3 tablespoons (45 ml) olive oil
1 medium onion, minced
8 *chiles poblanos,* roasted, peeled, seeded, deveined and chopped, or
    12 canned, peeled green chilies, chopped
6 ounces (175 g) tomatoes, peeled, seeded and minced
1 cup (250 ml) heavy cream
1 cup (250 ml) shredded Monterey Jack cheese
Salt and ground white pepper to taste

In a heavy skillet, heat the olive oil, then add the onion and cook and stir until translucent. Add the chilies and tomatoes and cook until slightly thickened, 3 or 4 minutes. Stir in the cream and cook several minutes longer, until heated through. Add the cheese and cook just until the cheese melts. Lightly stir in salt and pepper to taste and serve in a bowl over a warmer or in a chafing dish, if possible. Serve with hot tortillas.

SOUPS

SOUPS *(Sopas)*

Soups are among the glories of Mexican cooking. Beside being delicious, Mexican soups have less obvious qualities, as listed in this proverb: "Soup has seven virtues: it silences hunger, provokes little thirst, makes one sleepy, also patient, always pleasant, never angry, and gives a flush to the face."

SOPA DE AGUACATE
Avocado Soup

A smooth green soup to serve hot or cold.

Serves 6 to 8
4 tablespoons (60 ml) butter
2 tablespoons (30 ml) flour
8 cups (2 L) hot chicken broth
5 medium avocados, peeled and seeded
1 tablespoon (15 ml) minced onion
1/4 to 1/2 cup (75 to 125 ml) heavy cream
Salt and ground white pepper to taste
2 corn tortillas
2 tablespoons (30 ml) corn or safflower oil

In a large saucepan, heat the butter until it bubbles, then stir in the flour and continue to stir and cook for 2 to 3 minutes; do not allow the flour to brown. Stir in the broth, very slowly at first, and cook at a slow boil until it is slightly thickened; set aside. Mash the avocados with a fork or purée in a blender. Stir or blend 1 cup (250 ml) broth into the puréed avocados, then add this mixture to the broth in the saucepan. Add the onion and cream to the pan, season to taste with salt and pepper and simmer to blend the flavors. Meanwhile, cut each tortilla into 1-inch (3 cm) squares. In a small skillet, heat the lard or oil to the smoking point and fry the tortilla squares until crisp and golden; drain on absorbent paper. Pour the soup into a tureen or individual soup bowls and sprinkle the tortilla squares over the soup just before serving.

Note This soup can be chilled and served cold, with or without the tortilla squares. Or omit both the cream and tortilla squares and serve the cold soup with a spoonful of sour cream and a sprinkling of minced cilantro for each serving.

SOPA DE ELOTE
Corn Soup

A lovely, fresh soup.

Serves 6 to 8
4 tablespoons (60 ml) butter
1 small onion, minced
6 ounces (175 g) tomatoes, peeled, seeded and
  puréed
6 ears of corn
8 cups (2 L) chicken broth
Salt and ground white pepper to taste
1/2 cup (125 ml) heavy cream

Heat the butter in a small saucepan and add the
onion and puréed tomato; cook over low heat until
the onion is tender. Cut the kernels from the ears
of corn, scraping the ears with the knife to collect
all the milky juice of the kernels. Purée half of the
kernels in a blender or a food mill (if you use a
blender, add enough chicken broth to make a
smooth purée). Place the puréed corn in a large
saucepan and stir in the chicken broth and the
onion and tomato mixture; season to taste with
salt and pepper. Add the reserved corn, bring to a
boil, reduce heat and simmer about 15 minutes, or
until the soup has thickened slightly. Add the
cream and simmer a few minutes longer; taste and
adjust seasoning and serve.

SOPA DE FLORES DE CALABAZA
Squash Blossom Soup

If you can't find squash blossoms in a market,
gather them from a garden—to guard the squash
crop, take mostly mature male blossoms; female
blossoms have a miniature squash at the center.

Serves 6 to 8
1 pound (500 g) squash blossoms, stems and
  green bases removed
4 tablespoons (60 ml) corn or safflower oil
1 medium onion, minced
Salt
4 cups (1L) milk
4 cups (1L) chicken broth
4 tablespoons (60 ml) butter
2 tablespoons (30 ml) flour
Salt and ground white pepper to taste
1/2 cup (125 ml) heavy cream
2 egg yolks, beaten
4 thick slices good white bread, trimmed of
  crusts and cut into 1-inch (3 cm) cubes

Chop the squash blossoms coarsely. In a large saucepan, heat 1 tablespoon (15 ml) of the oil and add
the onion and the chopped blossoms. Sprinkle the
mixture lightly with salt, cover the saucepan and
cook over low heat until tender, about 15 minutes.
Purée the mixture in a blender or food mill (if you

use a blender, add enough of the milk to make a smooth purée). In the same saucepan used earlier, bring the milk to a simmer and stir in the purée, then add the chicken broth; set aside.

In another large saucepan, heat the butter until it bubbles, then stir in the flour and cook, stirring, 2 to 3 minutes; do not allow the flour to brown. Add the milk-flower mixture gradually while stirring. Season the soup to taste with salt and pepper.

In a small bowl, mix the cream into the beaten egg yolks, add a few tablespoons of the hot soup and add the egg-cream mixture to the soup pan. Stir thoroughly, then place on low heat to simmer. In a heavy skillet, heat the remaining 3 tablespoons (45 ml) oil to the smoking point and fry the bread cubes quickly until just golden brown; drain on absorbent paper. Serve the soup with fried bread cubes sprinkled over.

Squash blossoms

CALDO MICHE
Catfish Soup

Serves 6 to 8

6 small *chiles poblanos,* roasted, peeled, seeded
    and deveined
6 cups (1.5 L) water
1-1/2 pounds (750 g) tomatoes, peeled and
    chopped
2 medium onions, chopped
3 garlic cloves, crushed
1 teaspoon (5 ml) crushed dried oregano
Chopped cilantro to taste
2 bay leaves
1 teaspoon (5 ml) salt
1 2-pound (1 kg) catfish, or any whole white-
    fleshed fish
3 green plums, sliced (optional)

Mince 3 of the chilies and cut the other 3 into halves; set aside. In a saucepan large enough to accommodate the fish, bring the water to a boil. Add the chilies, tomatoes, onions, garlic, oregano, cilantro, bay leaves and salt. Maintain the water at a boil until the onion is tender, then reduce to a simmer and lower the fish into the broth. Allow the fish to cook for 5 minutes, then carefully lift out the fish and remove its skin. (To help keep the fish in one piece, wrap it in cheesecloth tied at both ends with long strings, using the strings to lower the fish into and remove it from the broth.) Return the fish to the saucepan (wrapped again in cheesecloth, if you like), adding the plums as well, and cook at a simmer for 5 to 10 minutes or until the plums are tender and the fish flakes when tested with a fork. Remove the fish carefully, keeping it whole, remove the cheesecloth if you have used it, and serve the fish in a deep serving dish with the broth.

SOPA DE PESCADO A LA VERACRUZANA
Fish Soup Veracruz Style

Serves 4
2 pounds (1 kg) fish heads, bones and trimmings
6 cups (1.5 L) water
2 small onions
1 bay leaf
1 teaspoon (5 ml) salt
4 tablespoons (60 ml) corn or safflower oil
3 garlic cloves, chopped
1 pound (500 g) tomatoes, peeled, seeded and
  puréed
1 pound (500 g) firm-fleshed fish,
  cut in chunks
1 tablespoon (15 ml) white vinegar
1 teaspoon (5 ml) crushed dried oregano
Salt and freshly ground black pepper to taste
Minced *chiles serranos* or *jalapeños* to taste

Place the fish heads, bones and trimmings in a saucepan with the water, 1 onion, cut in half, the bay leaf and salt and cook uncovered over medium heat for 30 minutes. Meanwhile, chop the second onion, heat 2 tablespoons (30 ml) of the oil in a heavy skillet and cook the onion along with the garlic until the onion is translucent. Add the puréed tomatoes and cook and stir over medium heat about 5 minutes; set aside.

In a separate skillet, heat the remaining 2 tablespoons (30 ml) oil almost to the smoking point and fry the fish chunks quickly until they are opaque and flake when tested with a fork; remove from the pan with a slotted spoon and set aside. When the fish broth has cooked for 30 minutes, strain the broth into another large saucepan and add the onion-tomato mixture and the fried fish. Add the vinegar, oregano and salt and pepper to taste. Simmer for a few minutes to blend the flavors and serve with a bowl of minced chilies to sprinkle over.

Note If you cannot get the makings for the fish stock from a local fish store or fisherman, substitute 2 cups (500 ml) bottled clam broth mixed with 4 cups (IL) water; omit the 1 teaspoon (5 ml) salt.

SOPA DE LIMA
Lime Soup

The sour lime is native to Yucatán, but this soup is also delightful made with sweet limes. Add some lemon peel to provide more of a tang.

Serves 6 to 8
4 tablespoons (60 ml) lard or corn or safflower oil
1 small onion, chopped
6 ounces (175 g) tomatoes, peeled, seeded and chopped
1 small green bell pepper, seeded, deveined and chopped
8 cups (2 L) chicken broth
1 sour lime, or
   1 sweet lime and 2 strips lemon peel
3 chicken gizzards
6 chicken livers
Salt and freshly ground black pepper to taste
Melted lard or corn or safflower oil to 1/4 inch (6 mm)
6 to 8 stale corn tortillas, cut into very thin strips

Heat 2 tablespoons (30 ml) of the lard or oil in a small skillet and cook the onion, tomatoes and bell pepper until the onion is translucent. Place the vegetables in a large saucepan and add the chicken broth and the juice of one-half of the sour or sweet lime, reserving the lime peel. Bring the broth to a boil over medium heat and drop in the reserved lime peel, adding the strips of lemon peel if you are using a sweet lime. Lower the heat and remove the peel or peels, maintaining the soup at a simmer.

Cut the remaining lime half into thin slices and set aside. With a sharp knife, trim the gizzards of their sacs, then chop the gizzards and livers finely. In a heavy skillet, heat the remaining 2 tablespoons (30 ml) lard or oil to the smoking point and cook the chopped giblets quickly until very lightly browned; season to taste with salt and pepper and keep warm. In another skillet, heat the 1/4 inch (6 mm) melted lard or oil to the smoking point and fry the tortilla strips until golden, then drain on absorbent paper. Ladle the soup into individual soup bowls, sprinkling the hot tortilla strips on top. Place the chopped giblets in a serving bowl and serve, along with the lime slices, to be added to the soup at the table.

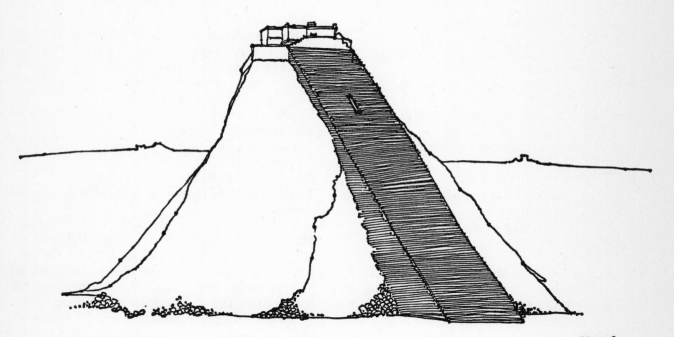

Uxmal

SOPA POBLANA
Pueblan Soup

A rich meat and vegetable soup.

Serves 6 to 8
2 tablespoons (30 ml) lard or corn or safflower oil
8 ounces (250 g) boneless pork loin, cut
  in small dice
1 medium onion, minced
Kernels cut from 3 ears of corn
3 small zucchini, diced
2 *chiles poblanos,* roasted, peeled, seeded,
  deveined and chopped
8 ounces (250 g) tomatoes, peeled, seeded,
  and puréed
8 cups (2 L) pork or chicken broth
Salt and freshly ground black pepper to taste
2 avocados, peeled and chopped
1/2 cup (125 ml) shredded *queso fresco* or
  Monterey Jack cheese

In a Dutch oven over medium heat, heat the lard or oil to the smoking point and add the diced pork. Cook and stir until the meat begins to brown, then cover and cook over low heat for 15 minutes. Add the onion, corn, zucchini and chilies to the pork, mix together well and add the tomatoes and broth. Season to taste with salt and pepper. Reduce heat and simmer, covered, until the vegetables are just tender. Just before serving, add the avocados and cheese, or pass the avocados and cheese in serving bowls to add to the soup at the table.

CHILEATOLE
Chicken and Corn Soup

A soup from Puebla to serve as a light meal with a salad and tortillas, or with a tortilla dish.

Serves 6 to 8
1 2-1/2- to 3-pound (1.25 to 1.5 kg) chicken,
  cut in serving pieces
Chicken broth (optional)
1 *chile ancho,* toasted, seeded and deveined
Kernels cut from 4 ears of corn
1 sprig *epazote* (optional)
1 large onion, chopped
1 teaspoon (5 ml) salt
1 teaspoon (5 ml) lard
2 tablespoons (30 ml) *masa harina*
1 teaspoon (5 ml) grated *piloncillo* or dark brown
  sugar

Place the chicken in a saucepan and add salted water to cover (use part chicken broth for a richer soup). Bring to a boil, then lower heat to a simmer and partially cover; cook for 30 minutes. Meanwhile, place the chili to soak in hot water to cover. When the chicken has cooked for 30 minutes, add the corn kernels, the *epazote,* onion and salt. Purée the chili in a blender, adding some of the broth from the chicken to make a smooth purée. Add the puréed chili and the lard to the chicken and simmer 10 to 15 minutes longer. Mix the *masa harina* with a little cold water and mix into the broth and, finally, add the *piloncillo.* Serve the soup in deep bowls, placing a piece of chicken and a spoonful of corn in each bowl along with some broth.

SOPA DE FRIJOL
Bean Soup

Serves 6 to 8
1/2 cup (125 ml) beans (pink, red, pinto or black)
4 cups (1 L) water
1 small onion, halved
4 tablespoons (60 ml) lard
2 cups (500 ml) reserved bean broth
6 cups (1.5 L) pork or chicken broth
8 ounces (250 g) tomatoes, peeled, seeded and
   puréed
2 teaspoons (10 ml) minced onion
1/2 teaspoon (3 ml) crushed dried oregano
Salt to taste
2 corn tortillas, cut in 1-inch (3 cm) squares
1/4 cup (75 ml) grated dry Monterey Jack or
   Parmesan cheese

Wash the beans and pick out any pebbles. Place them in a pot (preferably an earthenware pot) with the water and the onion. Bring the beans to a boil, add 1 tablespoon (15 ml) of the lard, then cover and reduce to a simmer. Cook until tender, about 1-1/2 hours. Drain the beans, reserving the broth. Purée the beans in a blender with the bean broth (or you may purée the beans in a food mill, then mix the purée with the broth). In the same pot in which the beans were cooked, mix the puréed beans with the pork or chicken broth and bring to a simmer.

In a small skillet, heat 1 tablespoon (15 ml) of the lard to almost smoking and add the tomatoes and onion; cook and stir over medium heat until the mixture thickens, 5 to 8 minutes. Add this sauce to the soup, along with the oregano and salt to taste. Keep warm.

In another skillet, heat the remaining 2 tablespoons (30 ml) lard to the smoking point and fry the tortilla squares until golden brown; drain on absorbent paper. Mix the grated cheese into the soup and serve in individual soup bowls with the tortilla squares sprinkled over, or pass the cheese and tortilla squares separately at the table.

Note 1-1/4 cups (325 ml) Frijoles Estilo Mexicano can be used in place of the dried beans.

SALADS

Jícamas

SALADS *(Ensaladas)*

Salads are perfect accompaniments to tortilla dishes and other *picante* entrées. Don't forget the simplest of Mexican salads: sliced tomatoes and/or avocados alone or on a bed of chopped romaine or leaf lettuce, or chopped lettuce with onion slices and radishes; for a dressing use a light oil and white vinegar mixture, or Salsa de Jitomate, and serve the salad on a separate plate or as a garnish for an entrée. Remember, also, that guacamole on a bed of chopped lettuce makes an excellent salad.

PICO DE GALLO
Jícama Salad

The crisp white flesh of the jícama makes a delightful salad ingredient with other vegetables, or mixed with oranges as in this recipe.

Serves 4
3 seedless oranges
1 large jícama
Salt and powdered *chile pequín* to taste

With a large sharp knife, cut the peel off of the orange down to the flesh, then cut just inside each white dividing membrane to make wedge-shaped sections. Peel the jícama with a small sharp knife or vegetable peeler and cut either in small dice or in thin slices about the same size as the orange sections. In a serving bowl, mix the jícama and orange sections together and season lightly with salt and powdered chili. Chill in the refrigerator for 30 minutes before serving. Pass a bowl of powdered chili with the salad, if you like.

ENSALADA DE NOPALITOS
Nopal Cactus Salad

Serves 6
2 pounds (1 kg) small nopal cactus joints, or
  2 cups (500 ml) canned *nopalitos,* drained
1 pound (500 g) tomatoes, peeled, seeded and
  chopped
3 tablespoons (45 ml) chopped onion
Chopped cilantro or oregano to taste
Chopped *chiles serranos* or *jalapeños* to taste
3 tablespoons (45 ml) corn or safflower oil
1 tablespoon (15 ml) white vinegar or more
Salt to taste
Crumbled *queso fresco* or natural cream cheese
  to taste

If you are using fresh nopal cactus pieces, scrape off the sharp spines and cut the cactus into very small strips or squares. Simmer the cactus in salted water to cover until tender, then drain in a colander. Hold the colander under cold, running water and rinse well to remove the sap released in cooking. In a mixing bowl, combine the tomatoes and cactus and add the onion, cilantro or oregano and chilies. Mix in the oil, vinegar and salt to taste. Place on a serving plate (preferably a glass plate) and chill in the refrigerator for about 30 minutes. Serve with the crumbled cheese sprinkled over.

ENSALADA DE COLIFLOR
Cauliflower Salad

Serves 4
1 small cauliflower
1 teaspoon (5 ml) dry mustard
2 tablespoons (30 ml) fresh orange
   juice or to taste
1 egg yolk
2/3 cup (150 ml) corn or safflower oil
1 *chile jalapeño,* seeded and minced
2 tablespoons (30 ml) white vinegar
Salt and ground white pepper to taste
1/2 teaspoon (3 ml) crushed dried oregano

Cook the cauliflower in a small amount of boiling salted water until just tender. Remove the cauliflower from the pan and drain in a sieve until cool, then separate it into flowerets. In a mixing bowl, dissolve the mustard in the orange juice, then beat in the egg yolk with a whisk. Add the oil slowly while beating with the whisk, then mix the remaining ingredients into the dressing; taste and adjust seasoning. Place the cauliflower in a shallow serving dish and pour the dressing over (or if you like, first place the cauliflower on a bed of chopped romaine lettuce leaves).

CALABACITAS EN VINAGRE
Marinated Zucchini

Serves 4
1 pound (500 g) small zucchini
3 tablespoons (45 ml) olive oil
4 garlic cloves, crushed
1 medium onion, cut in half
Salt and freshly ground black pepper to taste
Red wine vinegar
Crushed dried oregano or sage to taste
Thin slices of white or red onion, separated into
   rings (optional)

Trim the zucchini and cut into thin slices. In a large skillet, heat the olive oil, add the zucchini, garlic and onion and cook and stir 4 to 5 minutes over medium heat. Reduce heat to low, add salt and pepper and cover the skillet. Simmer the zucchini for 10 minutes, then uncover and allow to cook several minutes longer to evaporate any liquid in the skillet (more olive oil may be added at this point if necessary). Place the zucchini in a shallow dish and add wine vinegar to half cover. Sprinkle with oregano or sage and cover with aluminum foil. Refrigerate the zucchini for 4 to 5 days, stirring twice a day. Serve over a bed of chopped romaine lettuce leaves. Add thin slices of onions, separated into rings, if you like.

PESADUMBRE
Marinated Vegetable Salad

Serves 6 to 8
6 *chiles anchos*, toasted, seeded and deveined
1 garlic clove
A pinch of cumin seeds
1 cup (250 ml) white vinegar
2 pounds (1 kg) very small zucchini
1 pound (500 g) very small new potatoes
8 ounces (250 g) new green peas, shelled
1 sprig thyme
1 bay leaf
Salt to taste
1/2 white onion, separated into rings
1 teaspoon (5 ml) salt
1/4 cup (75 ml) olive oil
Slices of Monterey Jack or natural cream cheese

Soak the chilies in hot water to cover for 30 minutes. Drain and cover again with hot water, allowing them to soak overnight. The next day, drain the chilies and purée them with the garlic in a blender. Grind the cumin seeds in a mortar and add to the chilies. Add the vinegar to the chilies and blend to a smooth sauce. Cut the zucchini and potatoes into 1/2-inch (1 cm) slices. Cook the zucchini, the potatoes and the peas separately in small amounts of boiling salted water until just tender; drain. Combine the cooked vegetables in a bowl and add the chili mixture, thyme, bay leaf and salt to taste. In a separate bowl, place the onion rings and cover with cold water. Add the 1 teaspoon (5 ml) salt and mix. Cover both bowls tightly and chill several hours or overnight in the refrigerator. Just before serving, remove the bay leaf from the mixed vegetables and add the olive oil. Drain the onions. Place the mixed vegetables in a shallow serving dish and adorn with the onions and slices of cheese.

ENSALADA DE BETABEL
Beet Salad

Serves 4
4 medium beets
1/2 cup (125 ml) sherry
1 teaspoon (5 ml) sugar
1/4 teaspoon (2 ml) salt
1 tablespoon (15 ml) white vinegar
1 tablespoon (15 ml) chopped parsley

Cook the beets in boiling salted water to cover until just tender. Remove them from the pan and allow to cool, then peel and chop the beets into small dice and place in a mixing bowl. Mix together the sherry, sugar, salt and vinegar and stir into the beets. Adjust seasoning, cover and chill in the refrigerator 30 minutes or longer. Place in a shallow serving dish and sprinkle with chopped parsley.

EGG DISHES

EGG DISHES (Huevos)

The egg dishes served for the Mexican late break-fast *(almuerzo)* are perfect for brunch and supper, too; most of them are *picante* combinations of eggs, tomatoes and chilies. Serve with hot fresh flour or corn tortillas, fresh fruit, Chocolate en Leche or Café de Olla and a Mexican dessert such as Cajeta de Leche or Buñuelos.

HUEVOS RANCHEROS
Country-Style Eggs

Serves 3
1/2 cup (125 ml) lard or corn or safflower oil
1 small onion, chopped
1 garlic clove, minced
12 ounces (325 g) tomatoes, peeled, seeded and puréed
1 *chile serrano*, seeded, deveined and minced
Salt to taste
6 eggs
3 corn tortillas
4 ounces (125 g) Monterey Jack or natural cream cheese, thinly sliced
2 avocados, peeled and sliced (optional)

In a heavy skillet, heat 1 tablespoon (15 ml) of the lard or oil and cook the onion and garlic until the onion is translucent. Add the tomato purée and chili and simmer until the sauce thickens slightly.

Season to taste with salt and keep warm over low heat. In another heavy skillet, heat half of the remaining lard or oil and cook the eggs over low heat until the white is almost completely opaque, then turn the eggs carefully with a spatula to cook the tops for a few seconds. (Or you may baste the eggs with a spoon, tipping the pan slightly to collect the hot lard or oil). Carefully remove the eggs to a plate and keep them warm.

Add the remaining lard or oil to the second skillet and heat almost to the smoking point, then cook the tortillas until soft; do not brown. Place the tortillas on absorbent paper to drain, then place each tortilla in a heated individual casserole or on a heated plate. Top with 2 fried eggs, taking care not to break the yolks. Spoon the warm sauce over each egg and top with slices of cheese. Place under a broiler until the cheese is just beginning to melt, then garnish with avocado slices, if you like, and serve at once.

HUEVOS CAPORAL (Corporal's Eggs) Add 1 cup (250 ml) Frijoles Refritos to the above ingredients, spread each fried tortilla with a layer of refried beans, then top with eggs, sauce and cheese. Melt the cheese under a broiler and sprinkle with chopped cilantro to taste. Serve at once, omitting the avocados.

HUEVOS REVUELTOS CON SALSA
Scrambled Eggs with Sauce

Serves 3 to 4
2 *chiles poblanos,* roasted, peeled, seeded and
  deveined
2 tablespoons (30 ml) lard or corn or safflower oil
1 garlic clove, minced
1 tablespoon (15 ml) minced onion
1 pound (500 g) tomatoes, peeled, seeded and
  chopped
Chopped *chile serrano* to taste
2 tablespoons (30 ml) water
Salt and freshly ground black pepper to taste
6 eggs, beaten
1/4 cup (75 ml) shredded Monterey Jack cheese

Cut the *chiles poblanos* into small, thin strips. In a
heavy skillet, heat the lard or oil and fry the chilies
with the garlic and onion. When the onion is translucent, add the tomatoes, the *chile serrano* and the
water, and cook over medium heat, stirring, until
the sauce is slightly thickened. Season to taste with
salt and pepper. Lower the heat, add the beaten
eggs to the hot sauce, and cook and stir until the
eggs are barely set. Add the cheese and leave over
heat a few seconds longer until the cheese begins to
melt. Serve immediately on a heated serving dish.

Note This dish can be cooked without the chilies.

PISTO
Eggs Scrambled with Vegetables and Ham

Serves 4 to 6
8 ounces (250 g) peas, shelled
3 tablespoons (45 ml) lard or corn or safflower oil
4 ounces (125 g) ham, diced
6 small zucchini, diced
3 medium potatoes, cooked, peeled and diced
1 red or green bell pepper, minced
1 tablespoon (15 ml) minced onion
1 tablespoon (15 ml) minced parsley
6 eggs, beaten
Salt and freshly ground black pepper to taste

Cook the peas in boiling salted water to cover until
almost tender. Drain in a sieve or colander, pour
cold running water over, and set aside to drain
further. In a large, heavy skillet, heat the lard or oil
and fry the ham until lightly browned. Remove
from the skillet with a slotted spoon. In the same
lard or oil cook the diced zucchini for 1 or 2
minutes, stirring, then cover the skillet and cook
the zucchini on low heat for about 5 minutes, or
until almost tender. Add the potatoes and the bell
pepper and cook for 2 or 3 minutes, stirring carefully in order to keep the potatoes intact. Add the
onion and the parsley and continue to cook until
the onion is translucent. Add the eggs, peas and
ham and sprinkle with salt. Stir constantly until
the eggs are just beginning to set. Sprinkle with
pepper and serve at once.

HUEVOS EN RABOS DE MESTIZA
Eggs with Chili Strips

Serves 3
1-1/2 pounds (750 g) tomatoes, roasted
2 *chiles poblanos,* roasted, peeled, seeded and
    deveined
3 tablespoons (45 ml) corn or safflower oil
1 small onion, minced
Salt to taste
6 eggs
6 ounces (175 g) Monterey Jack or natural cream
    cheese, thinly sliced

Purée the roasted tomatoes in a blender; set aside. Cut the chilies into narrow strips about 2 inches (5 cm) long and set aside. In a heavy skillet, heat the oil and cook and stir the onion over low heat until the onion is translucent. Add the tomato purée and cook and stir over medium heat for 3 to 4 minutes; add salt to taste. Add the chili strips to the sauce and cook over reduced heat several minutes longer to blend the flavors. Break the eggs into the simmering sauce, then cover the pan and cook the eggs over low heat for about 5 minutes, or until the whites are set. Lay the slices of cheese over the eggs, cover the pan and cook 2 minutes longer or until the cheese is slightly melted. Serve at once in individual heated casseroles.

HUEVOS Y CREMA (Eggs and Cream) Reduce the amount of tomatoes in the preceding recipe to 1 pound (500 g), and cook and stir the tomato-onion mixture for 6 to 8 minutes, until slightly thickened. Add 3/4 cup (175 ml) heavy cream to the sauce and cook over medium heat 5 minutes longer, then add the chili strips and cook over reduced heat several minutes longer to blend the flavors. Break the eggs into the simmering sauce, then cover the pan and cook for about 7 minutes, until the eggs are just set. Place the eggs and sauce in individual heated casseroles, then divide 1/2 cup (125 ml) grated dry Monterey Jack or Parmesan cheese evenly over the casseroles and serve at once; omit the sliced cheese.

HUEVOS EN CHILE COLORADO
Eggs Cooked in Red Chili Sauce

Serves 3
1 *chile ancho*
3 *chiles pasillas*
2 pounds (1 kg) tomatoes, roasted
Salt to taste
2 tablespoons (30 ml) lard or corn or safflower oil
6 eggs
Grated dry Monterey jack or Parmesan cheese
   to taste

Toast the chilies lightly, then seed and devein (reserve a few chili seeds if you want a more *picante* sauce). Put the chilies and tomatoes into a blender and purée them to a smooth sauce, adding a small amount of water if necessary. Season with salt to taste. In a heavy skillet, heat the lard or oil and fry the chili sauce over medium heat for 3 to 4 minutes; add reserved chili seeds to taste, if you like. Break the eggs into the sauce, reduce heat to low, and cover and cook the eggs until set, about 5 minutes. Sprinkle with grated cheese to taste and serve immediately in heated individual casseroles or on heated plates.

HUEVOS EN CHILE VERDE
Eggs Cooked in Green Chili Sauce

Serves 2
2 *chiles jalapeños*
6 *tomatillos,* husked, or
   6 canned *tomatillos,* drained
2 tablespoons (30 ml) lard or corn or safflower oil
Salt to taste
4 eggs
Cilantro sprigs (optional)

Seed and devein the chilies, reserving some of the seeds if you want the sauce to be more *picante*. If you are using fresh *tomatillos,* cook them together with the chilies in salted boiling water to cover for 10 minutes, or until tender, then rinse in cold water and drain. If using canned *tomatillos,* cook the chilies in salted water until tender, rinse in cold water and drain. Blend the *tomatillos* and the chilies together in a blender, adding a small amount of water to make a smooth sauce. In a heavy skillet, heat the lard or oil and cook the chili sauce for about 5 minutes over medium heat, and then season to taste with salt. Add some of the reserved chili seeds to the sauce if you wish it to be more *picante*. Break the eggs into the sauce, reduce to a simmer, cover and cook the eggs until set, about 5 minutes. Serve immediately in individual heated casseroles or on heated plates, garnished with cilantro sprigs, if you like.

ROPA VIEJA
Shredded Beef with Eggs

Serves 4
2 pounds (1 kg) stewing beef
6 tablespoons (90 ml) lard or corn or safflower oil
1 small onion, minced
3 *chiles serranos,* seeded and minced
1 pound (500 g) tomatoes, peeled, seeded and
   chopped
Salt to taste
3 eggs, beaten

Cut the beef into small cubes and place in a large saucepan with salted water to cover. Bring to a boil, then reduce to a simmer and cook, partially covered, until the meat is tender, about 45 minutes to 1 hour. Cool the meat slightly in its broth, then drain and shred with a fork. In a large skillet heat 2 tablespoons (30 ml) of the lard or oil, add the onion and cook and stir until the onion is translucent, then add the chilies and tomatoes and cook over medium heat 2 to 3 minutes; add salt. In another large skillet, heat the remaining 4 tablespoons (60 ml) lard or oil almost to the smoking point, add the shredded beef and cook and stir until lightly browned. Add the chili-tomato mixture and simmer 2 to 3 minutes, then stir in the beaten eggs, continuing to stir until they are just set. Serve at once.

TORTILLA DISHES

AND TAMALES

ESSENCE AND PRESENCE OF CORN

The Mexican woman has employed corn in a manner as varied as it is intelligent and artistic. In no other part of America or of the world has corn been utilized in so many and such delicious forms.

In the tortillas, *soft and warm, as an inexhaustible bread.*

In the martajadas, *the* memelas, *the* tostadas, *the* lard gordas *and the sweet* gorditas.

In the tlachoyos *and the* quesadillas, *as rich as* empanadas.

In the enchiladas *and the green and red* chilaquiles, *with cheese on top and threads of meat wrapped inside.*

In the garnachas, tacos *and* chalupas, golosinas *so simple but so tasty.*

In the rich tortilla *soup and the elegant cream of corn.*

In the white atole *of the poor, so frugal and consoling to the stomach.*

In the strawberry atole *of our* tamal-*counters.*

In the exciting champurrado.

In the aromatic cinnamon pinole.

In the steamed tamales *of chile, of lard and of sweets exquisite in the mouth like a caress of foam.*

In the corn tamales, *with their chunks of* acitrón, *their raisins and their bluish spots.*

In the nutritious pozole *fragrant with oregano and perfumed with lime.*

In the fresh pozole, *sweet substance of corn from the hot earth.*

A thousand and one flavors, a thousand and one forms; all the best to attain the best, the most delicious, the most nutritious corn, though working hard and with the humblest implements: the metate, *the* molcajete, *the* comal, *the wooden spoons . . . with these the Mexican woman creates the greatest wonders.*

—C. Gandia de Fernández

Making corn tortillas

TORTILLA DISHES

Corn is the food on which the civilizations of Mexico were built, and although there is much more to Mexican food than the taco and the enchilada, the tortilla is still a basic ingredient of the cuisine. As is the case with most simple foods, the tortilla is at its best when it is most fresh. If you have ever eaten a hot handmade tortilla, you know that it is a very different thing from a machine-made, packaged, frozen and then defrosted and heated tortilla: The fresh tortilla has a fresher, more pronounced corn taste, and because it is thicker and not as uniform in thickness (or size) as a machine-made tortilla, the texture is slightly chewy and doughy at the same time. Fresh tortillas are, of course, preferable to frozen for all purposes, but they are put to their best uses when heated for tacos or eaten hot as a bread with meals; their superior flavor and texture are not as important for dishes calling for fried tortillas or tortillas covered with a sauce.

The best handmade tortillas are made from fresh *masa*, tortilla dough made by cooking and soaking dried corn in a mixture of unslaked lime and water to remove the husks and then grinding the softened corn to a smooth paste (traditionally on the *metate*). Handmade tortillas and fresh *masa* are usually available in areas of the United States with a sizable Mexican population.

If you do not have access to fresh tortillas and *masa*, you can make your own tortillas with *masa harina*, tortilla flour made from fresh *masa* and much more widely available. Though second in flavor and texture to tortillas made with fresh *masa*, tortillas made at home with *masa harina* will still be superior to frozen tortillas.

Frozen tortillas are perfectly adequate for any of the recipes in this book calling for tortillas; be sure that they are completely defrosted before using, however, and be sure to keep them covered while they are defrosting so that they will not dry out. You will need either fresh *masa* or *masa harina* for some dishes such as Sopes, Panuchos and Enchiladas de San Luis, which call for mixing other ingredients into the tortilla dough or molding the dough into special shapes.

Defrost frozen tortillas at room temperature or in an oven set on low heat. If the tortillas seem dry, wrap them in a damp cloth for several minutes before using, or brush them very lightly with water.

TORTILLAS
Corn Tortillas

Making tortillas is an art, and patting them out by hand is an art that may require more practice than most people are willing to devote to it, though it is fun to try. Pressing tortillas is easier, much like making pie dough. It does require a certain amount of experience, as you need to have a feel for the dough to know when it has reached the proper consistency for pressing. The first few times you use *masa harina*, it is wise to divide the dough into sections and then make one test tortilla before rolling all the sections into balls. If the dough is too wet or too dry, it can be adjusted by adding more flour or more water.

Makes 12 6-inch (15 cm) tortillas or
24 4-inch (10 cm) tortillas

1-1/2 pounds (1.75 kg) fresh *masa,* or
  2 cups (250 ml) *masa harina* mixed with
  1-1/4 to 1-1/2 cups (300 to 375 ml) warm water

If you are using *masa harina,* stir the water into the dough and mix well. Cover and let sit for 30 minutes.

To make 6-inch (15 cm) tortillas, divide the fresh *masa* or the dough made from *masa harina* into 12 equal sections and roll into 12 balls. If you want to pat the tortillas out by hand, wet your hands slightly, then pat each ball between palms and fingers, moving it gradually in a circular motion until it reaches about 6 inches (15 cm) in diameter. If you are pressing the tortillas, cut out 24 pieces of waxed paper or plastic wrap about 7 inches square (18 cm). Place one piece of paper or wrap on the bottom section of a tortilla press or other smooth surface, such as a table or a pastry board. Place a ball of dough in the center of the paper or wrap and cover with another paper or wrap; press with the top half of the tortilla press or with a flat board or flat bottom of a large saucepan. The tortilla should measure 6 inches (15 cm) in diameter. Peel off the top piece of paper or wrap and set the tortilla aside, then press 11 more tortillas, stacking them as they are pressed.

To make 4-inch (10 cm) tortillas, divide the dough into 24 sections and roll into balls. Cut out 48 pieces of waxed paper or plastic wrap about 5 inches (13 cm) square. Follow the preceding directions and press out 24 tortillas.

To cook, heat a lightly greased cast-iron griddle or skillet over medium heat. Place the tortilla on the palm or fingers of one hand, dough side down, and peel off the paper or wrap with the other hand. Place the tortilla on the hot griddle or skillet and cook until the dough begins to firm, then turn the tortilla over with a spatula and cook until lightly toasted—some dark spots will appear. Turn the tortilla once more, and cook until lightly toasted on the second side. At this point the tortilla should puff up slightly; if it does not, the heat is probably too high or too low and should be adjusted for cooking the remaining tortillas. Remove the tortilla from heat and keep warm in a basket lined with a cloth napkin, stacking the tortillas as you make them. If you plan to fill the tortillas, use the spotted side as the outside of the tortilla; it is slightly firmer than the more unblemished side.

TORTILLAS DE HARINA
Flour Tortillas

Flour tortillas are made with a rolling pin, like pie pastry. They are used for burritos and make a delicious hot bread to serve at dinner, spread with butter.

Makes 12 8-inch (20 cm) tortillas
3-3/4 cups (875 ml) all-purpose flour
1-1/2 teaspoons (8 ml) salt
1/2 cup (125 ml) lard or shortening
3/4 to 1 cup (175 to 250 ml) lukewarm water

Sift the flour and salt together. Cut the lard or shortening into the dry ingredients with a pastry cutter or work it in with your fingers. With a fork, stir in enough water to form a sticky mass. Knead the dough on a floured surface until smooth, about 2 or 3 minutes. Divide the dough into 2 equal pieces and form each into a ball. Cover the balls of dough with a moist cloth or plastic wrap and let sit at room temperature for 1 hour. With a rolling pin, roll out each ball of dough into a very thin circle on a floured board (the tortillas will shrink slightly as they cook). Cook on a lightly greased griddle or in a lightly greased skillet over medium heat until browned on the bottom, then turn and brown lightly on the other side. Stack the tortillas in a basket lined with a cloth, keeping them well covered, and serve hot.

Note If you are cooking the tortillas ahead, keep them tightly covered in a moist cloth or a plastic bag, and reheat by heating on a lightly greased griddle or in a lightly greased skillet, or by placing them in a covered container in a moderate oven— take care not to overheat them or they will dry out.

Tortilla basket

TOSTADAS

Tostadas are like open-faced sandwiches on fried tortillas rather than bread. They are the simplest of the *antojitos* but lend themselves to the most complex improvizations. Try any combination of foods you like, including hot foods and shredded lettuce, chopped tomatoes and shredded cheese, or just sprinkle a fried tortilla with shredded mild white cheese and place under a broiler for a little to melt the cheese; serve with Salsa de Jitomate. See Fillings for Tacos for other ideas.

TOSTADAS COMPUESTAS
Layered Tostadas

Makes 6
2 chicken breasts
Melted lard or corn or safflower oil to 1/4 inch (6 mm)
6 corn tortillas
1 cup (250 ml) Frijoles Refritos
1/2 cup (125 ml) diced *queso fresco* or Monterey Jack cheese
2 medium red potatoes, boiled in their jackets
3 tablespoons (45 ml) lard or corn or safflower oil
1 cup Guacamole, or
1 avocado, peeled and thinly sliced
1 small white onion, finely chopped
1/2 bunch romaine lettuce, shredded
3 tablespoons (45 ml) corn or safflower oil
1 tablespoon (15 ml) white vinegar
Salt to taste
Chiles chipotles in vinegar, drained, seeded and cut into small strips, to taste (optional)

Cook the chicken breasts in a small amount of salted water in a partially covered pan until just tender. Let cool, then skin, bone and shred with a fork; set aside.

In a heavy skillet, heat the lard or oil and fry the tortillas until almost crisp but still slightly soft in the center; drain on absorbent paper. Place the Frijoles Refritos in a saucepan, add the diced cheese and heat gently until the cheese begins to melt; remove from heat. Peel the potatoes and cut them into small cubes (or leave the peels on, if you like). In a heavy skillet, heat the 3 tablespoons (45 ml) lard or oil and lightly fry the potato cubes.

Assemble the tostadas in this order: First spread the tortillas with a spoonful of the beans and cheese, then some fried potatoes and chicken, then Guacamole or avocado slices. You can either put the onion and lettuce on in layers, mixing together the oil, vinegar and salt and sprinkling this mixture over the tostada and adorning it with *chiles chipotles,* or you can mix the onion and lettuce together and toss with the mixed oil, vinegar and salt, then top the tostada with this mixture and adorn the tostada with the chilies.

TACOS

Mexican tacos are quite different from the United States version of a taco, which is really more like a folded tostada.

Tortillas for tacos may be heated on both sides on a lightly greased griddle or in a lightly greased skillet; this is the simplest and most characteristic Mexican way of cooking them, and it is the best way to cook freshly made tortillas. To eat, fold them like a cigar rather than into a half-circle.

If tacos are fried they should be fried after they are filled, not before. Heat melted lard or corn or safflower oil to 1/4 inch (6 mm) in a heavy skillet over medium heat. Fill the tortillas, fold and fasten closed with a toothpick inserted vertically into the taco. Fry the taco lightly on one side, remove the toothpick and fry the taco on the other side; do not allow it to become more than slightly crisp—the tortilla should remain pliable.

Serve tacos immediately, with sauce to spoon inside. Extras such as chopped lettuce and tomatoes should be served and eaten separately as a garnish.

FILLINGS FOR TACOS

Tacos may, of course, be filled with almost any food. Following are some of the more obvious choices to combine as you like—look in the fish and vegetable sections for other ideas.

Filling for Panuchos de Picadillo
Filling for Burritos de Carne
Filling for Chiles Rellenos
Carnitas
Carne en Todo Junto
Cochinita Pibil
Crumbled fried *chorizo* sausage
Shredded cooked chicken, pork or beef, plain or fried
Frijoles Refritos
Sour cream
Shredded cheese
Chili strips

SAUCES FOR TACOS

Salsa de Jitomate
Salsa de Chile Pasilla
Salsa de Chipotle y Aguacate
Chile Frito
Guacamole

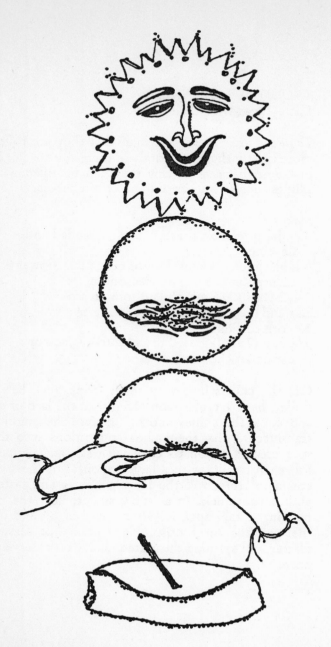

TACOS DE FRIJOLES CON CHORIZO
Tacos with Beans and Sausage

Makes 6
1 *chorizo* sausage
3 tablespoons (45 ml) lard or
   corn or safflower oil
1 cup (250 ml) Frijoles Estilo Mexicano
6 corn tortillas, preferably freshly made

Remove the casing from the *chorizo* and chop the *chorizo* or crumble it. Fry the *chorizo* in a skillet until it has browned and the fat has been rendered out. Leave the *chorizo* in its skillet. In another skillet, heat the lard or oil to the smoking point and fry the beans, stirring and mashing them into a paste (you may add some bean broth if you like). Transfer the bean paste to the skillet with the *chorizo* and cook and stir the mixture for several minutes, until well heated. Heat the tortillas on both sides on a lightly greased griddle or in a lightly greased heavy skillet. Place a heaping table-spoonful (15 ml) in the center of each hot tortilla, roll and serve at once on a heated platter.

Variation Drain the beans. Cook the beans with 1/2 onion, minced, until the onion is soft (do not mash the beans). Add 1 tomato, peeled and minced, 1 minced garlic clove and 1 *chorizo* sausage, finely chopped. Cook over medium heat until thickened and well heated. Fill hot tortillas and serve as above.

Making tacos

TACOS DE AGUACATE
Avocado Tacos

Makes 12
3 avocados, peeled
1 teaspoon (5 ml) hot prepared mustard
2 tablespoons (30 ml) heavy cream
1 tablespoon (15 ml) chopped cilantro or parsley
10 pitted green or black olives, chopped
Salt and freshly ground black pepper to taste
12 corn tortillas, preferably freshly made

Mash the avocados with a fork and add all the remaining ingredients except the tortillas; blend to a smooth paste. Heat the tortillas on both sides on a hot, lightly greased griddle or in a hot, lightly greased skillet, then fill and serve, or fill and fry lightly in 1/4-inch (6 mm) hot lard or oil; serve immediately.

TAQUITOS DE RAJAS
Little Tacos with Chili Strips

Taquitos are "little" tacos in that they are rolled more tightly than tacos and are therefore smaller in diameter; because of this they can be filled with fillings such as sour cream and cream cheese.

Makes 12
4 *chiles poblanos,* roasted, peeled, seeded and
    deveined
3 tablespoons (45 ml) lard or corn or safflower oil
1 tablespoon (15 ml) minced onion
1-1/2 cups (375 ml) chilled sour cream
Salt and ground white pepper to taste
12 corn tortillas
1/4 cup (75 ml) grated dry Monterey Jack or
    Parmesan cheese

Cut the chilies into very small strips. In a heavy skillet, heat 1 tablespoon (15 ml) of the lard or oil and cook the chilies and onion until the onion is translucent. Mix the chilies and onions into the sour cream; season to taste with salt and pepper. Fill each tortilla with a large spoonful of the sour cream mixture; roll the tortilla *tightly* and fasten with a toothpick. In a heavy skillet, heat the remaining 2 tablespoons (30 ml) lard or oil and fry the *taquitos* until crisp. Place on a hot serving platter and sprinkle the grated cheese over; serve at once.

BURRITOS

Burritos are a northern Mexico dish: Flour tortillas are filled, a small portion of the top and the bottom of the tortilla is folded over to hold in the filling, and the tortilla is then rolled like a cigar. Because flour tortillas are usually larger than corn tortillas, and because the method of folding the burrito is so effective in holding in the filling, several different kinds of filling can be used for each burrito. Try combinations of Frijoles Refritos, cheese, meat (see Fillings for Tacos) and various rice dishes (see Rice).

BURRITOS DE CARNE
Beef Burritos

Makes 12

Filling
3 pounds (1.5 kg) stewing beef
1 cup (250 ml) lard or corn or safflower oil
8 *chiles anchos,* toasted, seeded and deveined
6 garlic cloves
1/2 onion, coarsely chopped
Salt to taste

12 flour tortillas

Cut the beef into large cubes about 2 inches (5 cm) square. Pat the meat dry with absorbent paper. In a heavy skillet, heat 4 tablespoons (60 ml) of the lard or oil to the smoking point and brown the meat in small batches on all sides. Place the meat in a large saucepan. Add salted water to cover and bring to a boil, then reduce to a simmer and cook, partially covered, until the meat is tender, about 1-1/2 to 2 hours. Let the meat cool in its broth, then remove from the saucepan and shred with a fork; set aside. While the meat is cooling, soak the chilies in hot water to cover for 30 minutes, then drain and purée in a blender or food mill with 2 of the garlic cloves and the onion, adding enough water to make a smooth purée; add salt and set aside.

In a heavy skillet, heat the lard or oil almost to the smoking point. Crush 4 of the garlic cloves and cook, stirring, until the garlic begins to brown. Remove the garlic from the skillet and cook the shredded meat, stirring constantly, until it is well browned. Stir the chili purée into the meat and cook over low heat until thickened but still moist. Heat the tortillas one at a time on a lightly greased griddle or in a lightly greased skillet, filling each with a large spoonful of the meat-chili mixture, then fold and roll and serve immediately.

BURRITA NORTEÑA
Northern Burrito

Heat a lightly greased griddle or heavy skillet over medium heat. Place a flour tortilla on the griddle, place slices of Monterey Jack cheese over the tortilla, and place another tortilla on top. When the underside of the bottom tortilla begins to brown and become crisp, turn the double tortilla over. When the bottom of the second tortilla has begun to brown and crisp and the cheese is just melted, remove from the pan and fold as for a burrito. Serve plain or with Salsa de Jitomate, or sprinkle the slices of cheese with minced green chili.

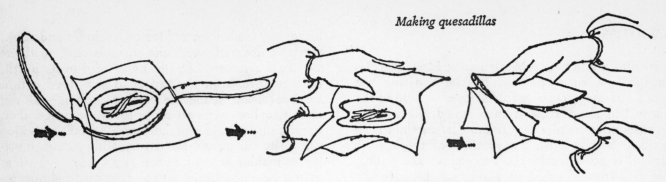

Making quesadillas

QUESADILLAS
Tortilla Turnovers

Quesadillas are turnovers made from raw tortillas that are filled and then heated or fried (though some *quesadillas* can be made from pre-cooked tortillas; see *Cheese* under Fillings for Quesadillas). They are quick to make once you master the technique of making your own tortillas; the filled *quesadillas* can be made ahead of time if they are kept tightly covered. *Quesadillas* should be served right after they are cooked as they are at their best when hot and fresh.

Makes 12
1 recipe Tortillas

Follow the recipe for Tortillas, making 12 balls of dough. Press or pat out the first tortilla, and place a spoonful of one of the following fillings on one-half of each raw tortilla. Fold in half, pressing the edges together to close the tortilla. Heat on both sides on a lightly greased hot griddle or in a lightly greased hot skillet for several seconds, or lightly fry on both sides in a heavy skillet with 1/4 inch (6 mm) melted lard or oil heated almost to the smoking point.

FILLINGS FOR QUESADILLAS

Cheese For each tortilla use a slice of any mild white cheese and thin strips of green chili. Cheese *quesadillas* can be made from pre-cooked tortillas —the melted cheese helps hold them closed. Place a tortilla on a hot griddle or in hot lard or oil in a skillet, lay a slice of cheese on top, place thin strips of green chili over the cheese, and when the cheese begins to melt fold the tortilla in half to finish cooking.

Meat Use any *picante* meat filling, such as Carne en Todo Junto, the filling for Panuchos de Picadillo or Burritos de Carne; or Carnitas or fried shredded cooked meat or chicken with a spoonful of sauce such as Chile Frito or Salsa de Jitomate; or shredded meat from a *picante* dish such as Cochinita Pibil. Also try crumbled fried *chorizo* sausage mixed with Frijoles Refritos.

Brains Soak fresh calve's brains in cold water to cover for 30 minutes; rinse. Place in a saucepan with salted water to cover, bring to a boil, reduce heat, cover and simmer for 10 to 15 minutes. Remove the brains and drain on absorbent paper, then chop. Cook chopped onion in a mixture of butter and corn or safflower oil. Add the chopped brains and cook and stir until lightly browned. Season with salt and minced *epazote* or freshly grated nutmeg to taste.

Squash Blossoms Cook chopped onion in corn or safflower oil and add squash blossoms, trimmed of stems and green bases and chopped. Season with minced green chili, salt and cilantro or *epazote*.

QUESADILLAS POTOSINAS
Priceless Tortilla Turnovers

In this recipe, puréed chilies are mixed with the tortilla dough.

Makes 12
2 *chiles anchos*, toasted, seeded and deveined
1 pound (500 g) fresh *masa*, or
    1-1/3 cups (325 ml) *masa harina*, mixed with
    1/2 to 3/4 cups (125 to 175 ml) warm water
Salt to taste
4 ounces (125 g) *tomatillos*, husked, or
    1/2 cup (125 ml) canned *tomatillos*, drained
1 or 2 *chiles serranos*, seeded and deveined
1 small onion, chopped
1-1/2 pounds (750 g) tomatoes, roasted
2 tablespoons (30 ml) lard or corn or
    safflower oil
2 cups (500 ml) shredded *queso fresco* or
    Monterey Jack cheese
1/2 cup (125 ml) grated dry Monterey Jack or
    Parmesan cheese

Soak the *chiles anchos* in hot water to cover for 30 minutes; drain. Purée the chilies in a blender and add to the fresh *masa;* add salt to taste. If you are using *masa harina,* add the water to the chilies in the blender to make a smooth sauce, then mix with the *masa harina* and add salt to taste.

If you are using fresh *tomatillos,* place them in a saucepan with the *chiles serranos* and the onion and cover with water; simmer until the *tomatillos* are tender, 10 to 15 minutes, then drain and purée in a blender or food mill with the roasted tomatoes. If using canned *tomatillos,* cook the onion and chilies until tender, then purée in a blender with the canned *tomatillos* and the roasted tomatoes. Heat the lard or oil and cook the purée over medium heat, stirring, until it is thickened. Remove from the heat and add the cheeses.

Divide the tortilla dough into 12 sections and shape into balls. Heat a lightly greased griddle or cast-iron frying pan, press or pat one ball of dough into a tortilla and cook the tortilla until the edges begin to crisp, then place a spoonful of the filling in the center of the tortilla and fold in half. At this point you can continue to cook the *quesadilla* on the griddle or in the pan, turning until it is nicely toasted; or the *quesadilla* can be fried in 1/4 inch (6 mm) hot melted lard or oil until it is golden. Proceed until all the *quesadillas* are cooked and serve them as quickly as possible.

Yanhutlán

ENCHILADAS

A general definition of the enchilada is a tortilla that has been dipped in sauce and is then rolled and eaten with a fork, though all dishes called enchiladas do not fit this definition, and some that do fit have other names. Thoroughly defrosted frozen tortillas are fine to use for enchiladas; be sure the tortillas are not dried out (cover them while defrosting and wrap in a damp cloth or brush lightly with water if necessary). Enchiladas should not be filled and then baked as is so often done in the United States; they are not a casserole dish but a dish that is assembled and served quickly so that the tortillas remain intact.

ENCHILADAS DE QUESO
Cheese Enchiladas

Serves 6

Sauce
4 *chiles anchos*, toasted, seeded and deveined
1 pound (500 g) tomatoes, roasted
2 tablespoons (30 ml) lard or corn or safflower oil
2 tablespoons (30 ml) minced onion
1 garlic clove, minced
Salt to taste

Melted lard or corn or safflower oil to 1/4 inch (6 mm)
12 corn tortillas
1-1/2 cups (375 ml) shredded Monterey Jack cheese
Minced white onion to taste (optional)

Soak the chilies in hot water to cover for 30 minutes, then drain, reserving the soaking water. Purée the chilies in a blender, adding enough reserved chili water to make a smooth purée. Add the roasted tomatoes and purée, adding more chili water to make a smooth sauce. In a heavy skillet, heat the 2 tablespoons (30 ml) lard or oil, add the onion and garlic and cook and stir until the onion is translucent. Add the tomato-chili sauce and cook and stir over medium heat for 6 to 8 minutes, until the sauce is thickened. Add salt to taste and keep the sauce warm over low heat. In another heavy skillet, heat the 1/4-inch (6 mm) lard or oil and cook the tortillas one at a time until they are softened but not browned. Drain the tortillas on absorbent paper very briefly, then dip each tortilla into the warm sauce, fill with a large spoonful of cheese (add minced onion, if you like), roll up and place in a heated serving dish seam side down. When all the tortillas are filled and rolled, pour the sauce over and serve at once.

ENCHILADAS DE POLLO (Chicken Enchiladas), ENCHILADAS DE CARNE (Beef or Pork Enchiladas) Follow the recipe for Enchiladas de Queso, substituting 1-1/2 cups (375 ml) shredded cooked chicken or meat for the cheese.

ENCHILADAS FINAS
Fine Enchiladas

These enchiladas are not filled, but are dipped in beaten eggs, then fried and dipped in sauce. An excellent side dish to serve with meats or chicken.

Serves 4 to 6

Sauce
3 *chiles mulatos* or *anchos,* toasted, seeded and
   deveined
1 garlic clove
3 tablespoons (45 ml) lard or corn or safflower oil
1 cup (250 ml) water
1 cup (250 ml) milk
Salt to taste

4 eggs, beaten
1/2 teaspoon (3 ml) salt
1 cup (250 ml) lard or corn or safflower oil
12 corn tortillas

Soak the chilies for 30 minutes in hot water to cover; drain. Purée the chilies with the garlic in a blender or food mill. In a heavy skillet, heat the lard or oil and fry the chili purée over high heat for several minutes, stirring constantly. Lower heat, add the water and milk and mix well. Season to taste with salt. Allow the sauce to simmer over a low heat. Meanwhile, combine the beaten eggs and the 1/2 teaspoon (3 ml) salt, mixing well. Heat the 1 cup (250 ml) lard or oil in a heavy skillet. Dip each tortilla in the egg batter, completely covering it on both sides with the batter, and fry on both sides in the hot lard or oil, turning very carefully. As each tortilla is fried, submerge it carefully in the simmering chili sauce, then fold in quarters or halves and place on a hot serving dish, until all 12 are dipped and folded. Serve immediately.

ENCHILADAS DE FLOR DE CALABAZA
Squash Blossom Enchiladas

If you cannot get squash blossoms from your garden or market, you might substitute the fruit of the blossoms: 1 pound (500 g) zucchini, crookneck or summer squash (cymlings). Grate the trimmed, unpeeled squash, salt lightly and leave in a colander for 30 minutes to drain; squeeze excess moisture from the grated squash by hand and use as directed for squash blossoms.

Serves 8
3 *chiles poblanos,* roasted, peeled, seeded and
    deveined
2 pounds (1 kg) tomatoes, peeled and chopped
1 garlic clove
4 tablespoons (60 ml) lard or corn or safflower oil
1 tablespoon (15 ml) chopped onion
1 packed handful of squash blossoms, trimmed
    of stems and green bases and chopped
8 ounces (250 g) *queso fresco* or
    Monterey Jack cheese
Melted lard or corn or safflower oil to 1/4 inch
    (6 mm)
16 corn tortillas

Purée the chilies together with half of the chopped tomatoes and the garlic clove in a blender or food mill. Heat 2 tablespoons (30 ml) of the lard or oil and cook the chili sauce over medium heat, stirring, for about 5 minutes (add a small amount of water if necessary to make a smooth sauce). Heat the remaining 2 tablespoons (30 ml) lard or oil and cook the onion until it is translucent. Add the chopped squash blossoms and cook and stir over medium heat for about 10 minutes; add the remaining chopped tomatoes and cook 5 minutes longer, until the mixture is thick. Remove from heat. Grate half of the cheese and add to the squash blossom mixture.

Heat the lard or oil and fry each tortilla lightly; do not allow the tortillas to become crisp. Dip each tortilla in the chili-tomato sauce, coating both sides. Fill with a large spoonful of the squash blossom mixture, fold in half and place on a hot ovenproof platter. Pour the remaining sauce over. Cut the remaining cheese in thin slices and place on top of the enchiladas. Put the platter in a preheated 350°F (180°C) oven until the cheese just begins to melt; serve immediately.

ENCHILADAS DE SANTA CLARA
Enchiladas of Santa Clara

Serves 8

Sauce
4 *chiles mulatos*
4 *chiles anchos*
1 teaspoon (5 ml) sesame seeds
1 clove
2 peppercorns
1/2 cinnamon stick
3 tablespoons (45 ml) lard or corn or safflower oil
Salt to taste

Filling
8 ounces (250 g) pork shoulder
3 tablespoons (45 ml) lard or corn or safflower oil
1 tablespoon (15 ml) chopped onion
1 garlic clove, chopped
1 teaspoon (5 ml) chopped parsley
8 ounces (250 g) tomatoes, peeled, seeded and
    puréed
1/4 cup (75 ml) slivered blanched almonds
1/4 cup (75 ml) pine nuts
1/4 cup (75 ml) golden raisins
1 tablespoon (15 ml) chopped *acitrón* or
    candied pineapple
Salt to taste

Melted lard or corn or safflower oil to 1/4 inch
    (6 mm)
16 corn tortillas
2 eggs, separated
A pinch of salt

Toast, seed and devein the chilies. Soak them in hot water to cover for 30 minutes; drain. Meanwhile, toast the sesame seeds by stirring them in a hot ungreased skillet; watch carefully so they do not burn. Purée the soaked chilies in a blender; grind the sesame seeds, clove, peppercorns and cinnamon stick together in a mortar or spice grinder; add to the chilies. In a skillet, heat the 3 tablespoons (45 ml) lard or oil and cook the chili mixture over medium heat, adding enough water to make a smooth sauce. Stir and cook the sauce until it thickens slightly; season to taste with salt and keep warm over low heat.

To make the filling, cook the pork in a small amount of water in covered pan until tender, let cool in its broth. Drain and shred. In a skillet, heat the 3 tablespoons (45 ml) lard or oil and fry the meat. When it begins to brown, add the onion, garlic, parsley, tomatoes, almonds, pine nuts, raisins and *acitrón* or pineapple; add salt to taste.

Heat the lard or oil in a skillet and fry each tortilla lightly, until it is softened but not browned. Dip each tortilla into the chili sauce, coating both sides of the tortilla. Fill the tortilla with a spoonful of the filling and roll it up. In a deep ovenproof casserole make a layer of enchiladas and cover with a second layer, then pour the remaining chili sauce over. Beat the egg yolks lightly. Beat the egg whites until stiff but not dry; incorporate the egg yolks bit by bit. Add a pinch of salt. Spread the beaten eggs over the layered enchiladas and place the casserole in a preheated 350°F (180°C) oven until the eggs are set; serve immediately.

ENCHILADAS SUIZAS
Swiss Enchiladas

A mild dish, without chilies, using fresh heavy cream rather than sour cream.

Serves 6
4 chicken breasts
2 pounds (1 kg) tomatoes, peeled, seeded and
  coarsely chopped
1 small onion, quartered
1 garlic clove
Salt to taste
1/2 cup (125 ml) corn or safflower oil
12 corn tortillas
1 cup (250 ml) heavy cream

Place the chicken breasts in a saucepan with salted water to cover, and simmer, partially covered, until tender. Allow the chicken to cool in its broth, then skin, bone and shred with a fork; set aside.

In a blender or a food mill, purée the tomatoes, onion and garlic; add salt to taste. In a heavy skillet, heat 2 tablespoons (30 ml) of the oil and cook and stir the tomato mixture over medium heat until it has thickened slightly, about 5 to 10 minutes. Taste and adjust seasoning. Set aside and keep warm. In another large skillet, heat the remaining oil almost to the smoking point and cook the tortillas one at a time until they are softened but not browned. Drain the tortillas on absorbent paper very briefly, then fill each with a spoonful of shredded chicken, roll up and place in a heated serving dish, seam side down. When all the tortillas are filled and rolled, pour the tomato sauce over. Pour the heavy cream over and serve at once.

PAN DE CAZÓN
Fish Tortillas

In Campeche, this dish of tortilla "sandwiches" would be made with *cazón*, which is a small shark. Any firm-fleshed fish, such as halibut or swordfish, can be substituted. Although the character of the dish will be different, cilantro may be used if *epazote* is unavailable.

Serves 6

Filling
2 cups (500 ml) water
1 onion slice
A pinch of salt
1 pound (500 g) halibut or swordfish steaks
4 tablespoons (60 ml) lard or corn or safflower oil
1 tablespoon (15 ml) minced onion
1 teaspoon (5 ml) chopped *epazote*

Sauce
2 pounds (1 kg) tomatoes, peeled, seeded and chopped
1 *chile serrano*, seeded (if desired) and chopped
1/2 cup (125 ml) lard or corn or safflower oil
1 medium onion, sliced
1 sprig *epazote*, chopped
Salt to taste
1/2 cup (125 ml) water

Bean Paste
1 recipe Frijoles Estilo Mexicano, using black beans and 4 cups (1 L) water
4 tablespoons (60 ml) lard or corn or safflower oil
1 medium onion, chopped
1 sprig *epazote*
Salt to taste

12 corn tortillas

Place the water, onion slice and salt in a large saucepan and bring to a boil. Add the fish, cover the pan partially and reduce heat to a simmer; cook for 5 to 10 minutes, or until the fish flakes

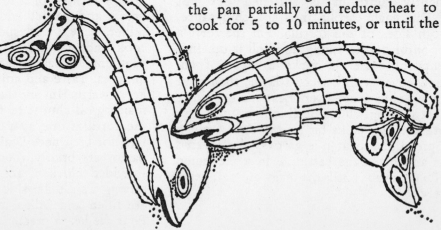

when tested with a fork. Allow to cool slightly in the liquid, then remove from the pan, remove any skin and bone and shred the fish with a fork. In a heavy skillet, heat the lard or oil and add the onion and *epazote,* then add the shredded fish. Cook over low heat until heated through; do not allow it to brown. Set aside and keep warm.

To make the chili sauce, purée the tomatoes and the chili in a blender or food mill. In a heavy skillet, heat the lard or oil almost to the smoking point, then add the tomato-chili mixture with the onion and the *epazote.* Cook and stir over medium heat 5 to 10 minutes, or until the mixture thickens. Add the water and simmer several minutes longer. Season to taste with the salt; set aside and keep warm.

To make the bean paste, place the beans, along with their broth, in a blender (in batches, if necessary) and blend to a purée (or purée the beans in a food mill). In another heavy skillet, heat the lard or oil to the smoking point and add the beans, onion and *epazote* and cook and stir over medium heat until the beans are thickened. Season to taste with salt; set aside and keep warm.

Dip each tortilla (unfried) in the warm chili sauce, making sure both sides are well covered, and place on a hot platter. Spread a thick layer of bean paste over the tortilla, then a layer of fried fish. Dip another tortilla in the chili sauce; place on top of the layer of fish. Continue to assemble the tortillas in pairs, working quickly so they do not cool off, and when all are assembled pour a spoonful of sauce over each "sandwich" and serve immediately. Serve with guacamole, if you like.

FLAUTAS DE POLLO
Chicken Flutes

Flautas are rolled tightly, like *taquitos,* then fried crisply and covered with a sauce.

Serves 6 to 8
1 2-1/2 pound (1.25 kg) chicken, cut into serving
   pieces
4 cups (1 L) chicken broth or more
24 corn tortillas
Melted lard or corn or safflower oil to 1/4 inch
   (6 mm)
1 recipe Salsa de Tomate Verde Cocida
Shredded Monterey Jack cheese to taste (optional)
Sour cream to taste (optional)

Place the chicken in a saucepan with the chicken broth, bring to a boil, then reduce heat, partially cover and simmer until tender, 30 to 45 minutes. Allow the chicken to cool in its broth, then skin, bone and shred with a fork.

Heat the tortillas briefly on a lightly greased griddle or in a lightly greased skillet, then place a spoonful of chicken along one edge of each tortilla and roll up very tightly. Fasten each rolled tortilla with a toothpick. In a heavy skillet, heat the lard or oil to the smoking point and fry the rolled tortillas until crisp and golden, then drain them briefly on absorbent paper. Place the *flautas* on a heated serving dish, cover with the sauce, add cheese and/or sour cream, if you like, and serve immediately.

TAQUITOS DE QUESO
Little Cheese Tacos

Though called *taquitos,* these have sauce poured over, like *flautas.*

Makes 12
2 *chiles poblanos,* roasted, peeled, seeded, deveined and chopped
8 ounces (250 g) tomatoes, peeled, seeded and chopped
3 tablespoons (45 ml) lard or corn or safflower oil
1 tablespoon (15 ml) minced onion
Salt to taste
12 corn tortillas
12 ounces (325 g) Monterey Jack or natural cream cheese
1/2 cup (125 ml) sour cream, mixed with
1/4 cup (75 ml) buttermilk, or
    3/4 cup (175 ml) heavy cream

Purée the chilies and the tomatoes in a blender or food mill. In a heavy skillet, heat 1 tablespoon (15 ml) of the lard or oil and cook the onion until it is translucent. Add the chili-tomato purée and cook and stir over medium heat until slightly thickened; season with salt to taste and keep warm over low heat. In another heavy skillet, heat the remaining 2 tablespoons (30 ml) lard or oil and fry the tortillas lightly, not allowing them to become crisp; drain briefly on absorbent paper. Cut the cheese into 12 long, narrow strips and place 1 strip on the outer edge of each tortilla and roll up tightly. Place on a hot serving platter and cover with the chili-tomato sauce. Pour over the sour cream-buttermilk mixture or the heavy cream and serve at once.

PANUCHOS DE PICADILLO
Stuffed Tortillas

One of the seemingly infinite variations of the tortilla is the *panucho,* a tortilla cooked to be hollow and then stuffed. The *panuchos* may be stuffed and kept tightly covered for several hours; fry them at the last minute. See Fillings for Tacos for other stuffing suggestions.

Makes 12

Filling
2 tablespoons (30 ml) lard or corn or safflower oil
8 ounces (250 g) finely chopped beef
1 tablespoon (15 ml) chopped onion
8 ounces (250 g) tomatoes, roasted and puréed
2 teaspoons (10 ml) chopped parsley
1 tablespoon (15 ml) golden raisins, soaked in water to plump
1 tablespoon (15 ml) slivered blanched almonds
Salt to taste

1 recipe Tortillas
1 cup (250 ml) Frijoles Refritos
Melted lard or corn or safflower oil to 1/4 inch (6 mm)

To make the filling, in a heavy skillet heat the lard or oil to the smoking point and cook the meat and onion until the meat is browned. Add the puréed tomatoes and parsley and cook and stir over medium heat about 10 minutes, until thickened. Add the raisins and almonds and season with salt to taste.

Pat or press out 12 tortillas. As each tortilla is

turned for its final toasting, spotted side up, it should puff up. If not, tap it lightly with your fingertips or press gently with a spatula to make it puff. As the tortillas cool, with a small knife cut a slit in one edge of each tortilla large enough to allow it to be stuffed. Spread a layer of beans inside each tortilla, then spread the beans with a layer of filling. When all the *panuchos* are filled, in a heavy skillet heat the 1/4 inch (6 mm) lard or oil and fry them lightly, draining them briefly on absorbent paper. Serve with Salsa de Jitomate or another table sauce, or serve with a cooked sauce such as Chile Frito poured over.

Making panuchos

SOPA SECA DE TORTILLA
"Dry Soup" Casserole

On festive occasions in Mexico, a "dry soup" course, consisting of a bland, starchy dish, follows the "wet" soup course. This filling dish can also serve as an entrée along with a vegetable dish or a salad.

Serves 4 to 6
1/2 cup (125 ml) lard or corn or safflower oil
1 medium onion, minced
1 garlic clove, minced
1 pound (500 g) tomatoes, peeled, seeded and puréed
Salt and freshly ground black pepper to taste
12 stale corn tortillas, cut into thin strips
1 cup (250 ml) sour cream
3/4 cup (175 ml) shredded Monterey Jack cheese
1 tablespoon (15 ml) butter

In a large skillet, heat 1 tablespoon (15 ml) of the lard or oil and add the onion, cooking it until it is translucent. Add the garlic and the puréed tomatoes and cook and stir until slightly thickened, 5 minutes or more. Season to taste with salt and pepper; set aside and keep warm. In another large skillet, heat the remaining lard or oil almost to the smoking point and fry the tortilla strips lightly, taking care not to brown them. Remove the strips from the pan with a slotted spoon and drain briefly on absorbent paper. Lightly butter an ovenproof casserole and place in it the following ingredients in layers: tortilla strips, tomato sauce, sour cream and shredded cheese, ending with a layer of cheese. Dot evenly with butter and place in a preheated 350°F (180°C) oven for about 25 minutes, or until lightly browned on top.

Variation Four *chiles poblanos* that have been roasted, peeled, seeded, deveined and cut into strips may be added to cook with the garlic and the tomato purée.

BUDÍN AZTECA
Aztec Pudding

Serves 4
2 chicken breasts
4 *chiles poblanos,* roasted, peeled, seeded and
    deveined
2 tablespoons (30 ml) lard or corn or safflower oil
4 tablespoons (60 ml) minced onion
1-1/2 pounds (750 g) tomatoes, peeled, seeded and
    puréed
Salt to taste
4 eggs, separated
Melted lard or corn or safflower oil to 1/4 inch
    (6 mm)
8 corn tortillas
2 cups (500 ml) shredded Monterey Jack cheese

Cook the chicken breasts in salted water to cover in a partially covered saucepan until tender; allow the chicken breasts to cool in the broth, then skin, bone and shred with a fork; set aside.

Cut the chilies into thin strips and set aside. In a heavy skillet, heat the 2 tablespoons (30 ml) lard or oil and cook and stir the onion until it is translucent. Add the puréed tomatoes and cook and stir over medium heat for about 5 minutes, or until slightly thickened; add salt and set aside.

Beat the egg yolks slightly, then beat the egg whites until stiff and fold in the beaten yolks. In a heavy skillet, heat the 1/4 inch (6 mm) lard or oil to the smoking point. Dip a tortilla into the eggs to coat both sides, then fry in the hot lard or oil until golden brown. Place the tortilla in a round casserole and sprinkle with chilies, chicken, a large spoonful of sauce and some cheese, then dip and cook a second tortilla and continue to layer, ending with a tortilla. Pour any remaining egg over the top of the pudding and place in a 350°F (180°C) oven until golden brown, about 20 minutes. Serve immediately.

ENCHILADAS DE SAN LUIS
Enchiladas of San Luis

From San Luis Potosí, this dish is really a tortilla casserole made with filled and folded tortillas; the tortillas must be made from scratch as powdered chilies and grated cheese are mixed into the dough.

Serves 6
4 *chiles anchos,* toasted, seeded and deveined
1-1/2 pounds (750 g) fresh *masa,* or
   2 cups (250 ml) *masa harina* mixed with
   1-1/4 to 1-1/2 cups (300 to 375 ml) warm water
1 cup (250 ml) grated dry Monterey Jack or
   Parmesan cheese
4 tablespoons (60 ml) lard or corn or safflower oil
1 large onion, chopped
1-1/2 pounds (750 g) tomatoes, peeled, seeded
   and chopped
6 *chiles poblanos,* toasted, peeled, seeded,
   deveined and chopped
1-1/2 cups (375 ml) shredded *queso fresco* or
   Monterey Jack cheese
1 small head romaine lettuce
4 tablespoons (60 ml) butter

Grind the chilies to a powder in a blender and mix into the fresh *masa* or the *masa harina* and water mixture. Add the grated cheese, mixing well. (If you are using *masa harina,* allow the dough to sit, covered, for 30 minutes.) Make 12 tortillas, following the instructions in the recipe for Tortillas. Stack the tortillas and set them aside, covered with a cloth.

In a heavy skillet, heat the lard or oil and cook the onion until it is translucent. Add the chopped tomatoes and the chilies and cook and stir over medium heat for about 5 minutes, until thickened. Remove from heat, add the shredded cheese, mixing it in gently; set aside.

Line a deep, ovenproof casserole with half of the lettuce leaves. Fill half the tortillas with spoonfuls of the chili mixture, fold them in half and arrange them over the lettuce leaves. Heat the butter gently until it just begins to brown; dribble half of the browned butter over the folded tortillas. Fill and fold the remaining tortillas and arrange them over the first layer of tortillas; dribble the remaining browned butter over. Cover with the remaining lettuce leaves and cover the casserole with a tightly fitting lid. Place the casserole in a larger pan and add hot water to the larger pan to a depth of 2 inches (5 cm). Bake in a preheated 350°F (180°C) oven for 20 minutes; serve, in the casserole dish, at once.

CHILAQUILES
Tortilla Casserole

Serves 4 to 6
16 stale corn tortillas
Melted lard or corn or safflower oil to 1/2 inch
   (1 cm)
1 pound (500 g) *tomatillos,* husked, or
   2 cups (500 ml) canned *tomatillos,* drained
3 *chiles serranos,* seeded and deveined
2 *epazote* leaves (optional)
3 sprigs cilantro
2 onions, chopped
1 tablespoon (15 ml) lard or corn or safflower oil
1 cup (250 ml) shredded *queso fresco* or
   Monterey Jack cheese
1 cup (250 ml) hot chicken broth
A handful of small radishes, sliced or cut into roses
Chopped cilantro to taste

Cut the tortillas into narrow strips. Heat the lard or oil and fry the tortilla strips until they are golden but not brown. Remove the tortilla strips and drain them on absorbent paper. If using fresh *tomatillos,* cook them in boiling salted water to cover until tender, about 10 minutes. Purée the *tomatillos* in a blender or food mill together with the chilies, the *epazote,* cilantro and one-half of the chopped onions. Heat the 1 tablespoon (15 ml) of lard or oil and cook the purée for several minutes over high heat, stirring constantly.

Grease a flameproof casserole and make a layer at the bottom with half of the tortilla strips. Place half of the cheese in a layer over the tortilla strips. Cover the cheese with half of the remaining chopped onions, then half of the *tomatillo* sauce. Repeat the layers of tortillas, cheese, onions and sauce, then pour the hot chicken broth over. Cook over low heat until the tortilla strips are very soft and the cheese is melted, about 20 minutes. Serve at once, garnished with radishes and chopped cilantro, if you like.

CHILAQUILES ESTILO GUERRERO
Tortilla Casserole Guerrero Style

A quick and delicious way to use up leftover tortillas.

Serves 4
1 pound (500 g) tomatoes, peeled, seeded and
   chopped
3 *chiles serranos,* seeded, deveined and chopped
8 to 12 stale corn tortillas
4 tablespoons (60 ml) butter
Salt to taste
1/2 cup (125 ml) sour cream
1/2 cup (125 ml) shredded *queso fresco* or
   Monterey Jack cheese

Purée the tomatoes and the chilies together in a blender or food mill. Cut the tortillas into quarters. In a heavy skillet, melt the butter and cook the tortilla pieces until crisp but not brown. Add the tomato-chili mixture and cook over a medium flame about 5 minutes, until the tortilla pieces begin to soften slightly. Add salt to taste and serve immediately, bathed with the sour cream and shredded cheese.

TAMALES

Tamales are made in the home for special occasions—because they are time-consuming to prepare they are not considered everyday food. They are made from a corn flour especially made for tamales. If you cannot find *harina de tamal* you may substitute *masa harina*—tortilla flour—but the *tamal* dough will be heavier and coarser by comparison. An electric mixer is a great help in mixing the *tamal* dough.

Buy the corn husks in a Mexican market, or make your own dried corn husks by simply allowing fresh husks to dry in the sun or in an oven on very low heat. Trim for use for tamales by cutting off the tops and bottoms of the leaves to make a flat leaf with squared ends.

Dried corn husks (about 40 if husks are wide,
　more if they are narrow)
1 cup (250 ml) lard
1/2 teaspoon (3 ml) baking powder
1-1/2 teaspoons (8 ml) salt
1 pound (500 g) *harina de tamal,* or
　4 cups (1 L) *masa harina*
1-1/2 cups (375 ml) lukewarm chicken broth

The morning of the day you prepare the tamales, place the corn husks in hot water to cover and allow them to soak for 3 hours or more. After the leaves have soaked, drain them and dry well on absorbent paper. Tear enough husks into narrow strips to make 36 strips to be used in tying the tamales closed; set aside.

To make the tamales, beat the lard in a large bowl with a whisk or an electric mixer for 5 minutes or longer, or until it is light and spongy. Mix the baking powder and salt into the flour, then gradually add 1 cup (250 ml) of the flour into the lard, beating constantly. Add 1/2 cup (125 ml) chicken broth *very slowly,* beating constantly. Continue to alternate adding cupfuls of flour with half-cups of broth, beating constantly, until both are completely mixed into the lard. Beat the mixture 3 to 4 minutes longer. To test for doneness, roll a small amount of the *tamal* dough into a ball and place it gently in a glass of cold water. When the ball of dough floats, the dough is ready.

Spread a spoonful of dough evenly in a rectangle about 1/8 inch (3 mm) thick in the center of the inside of each husk, slightly closer to the broad end rather than the pointed end. If the husk is too narrow, use 2 overlapping husks. Leave enough empty space at the sides and the ends of the husk to fold over the dough—an area about twice the size of the dough rectangle. Spread a small spoonful of filling down the center of the dough rectangle. Fold in the sides of the husk, fold over the pointed end and then the broad end. Tie a strip of corn husk across the top flap to close the *tamal.* Stack the tamales, not too tightly, in a steamer, seam sides down, cover tightly and steam for 1 hour. To test for doneness, open one *tamal;* the dough should be light in texture and cooked through.

Tamales may be frozen and then reheated in a covered casserole in a medium oven. They may also be reheated from room temperature by toasting on a griddle or in a frying pan.

FILLINGS FOR TAMALES

Any *picante* filling may be used for tamales: a combination of shredded cooked chicken or meat mixed with a chili sauce, or a filling of chicken or meat and sauce cooked together. The following recipes make excellent fillings; see the sections on Meat and Birds for other ideas.

Shredded cooked chicken, pork or beef, mixed with one of the following:

    Chile Frito
    Salsa de Tomate Verde Cocida
    Sauce for Enchiladas de Queso
Carne en Todo Junto
Filling for Panuchos de Picadillo
Filling for Burritos de Carne
Filling for Chiles Rellenos
Cochinita Pibil
Lomo de Cerdo Adobado
Lomo de Cerdo en Chile Verde
Pierna de Carnero Enchilada
Mole de Pavo
Mole Poblano

TAMALES DE DULCE (Sweet Tamales) Follow the recipe for Tamales, adding 3/4 cup (175 ml) sugar to the *tamal* dough, and reducing the amount of salt to 1/2 teaspoon (3 ml). Fill the tamales with strips of coconut, raisins, nuts, jams, or diced fresh or candied fruits.

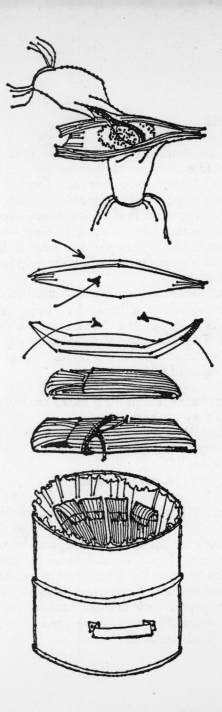

Making tamales

TAMALES DE POLLO
Chicken Tamales

Makes 36

Filling
1 3- to 3-1/2-pound (1.5 to 1.75 kg) chicken, cut
    into serving pieces
2 *chiles anchos,* toasted
1 *chile pasilla,* toasted
4 tablespoons (60 ml) lard or corn or
    safflower oil
1 slice good white bread
1 corn tortilla
1 tablespoon (15 ml) slivered blanched almonds
1 tablespoon (15 ml) pumpkin seeds
1 teaspoon (5 ml) sesame seeds
1/2 teaspoon (3 ml) reserved chili seeds
1 medium onion, roughly chopped
1 garlic clove
2 cloves
1 peppercorn
1/2 cinnamon stick
1 cup (250 ml) reserved chicken broth
Salt to taste

1 recipe Tamales

Place the chicken pieces in a saucepan with salted water to cover and bring to a boil, then reduce heat, partially cover, and simmer until the chicken is tender, about 45 minutes. Allow the chicken to cool in its broth, then remove from the pan, skin and bone the chicken and shred the meat with a fork. You may boil the broth to concentrate it, if you like. Reserve the broth. While the chicken is cooking, seed and devein the chilies, reserving 1/2 teaspoon (3 ml) of the *chile ancho* seeds. Cover the chilies with hot water and soak for 30 minutes; drain.

When the chicken is cooked and shredded, in a heavy skillet heat 2 tablespoons (30 ml) of the lard or oil and fry the slice of bread lightly on both sides; remove to drain on absorbent paper. Fry the tortilla in the same lard or oil until golden; remove and drain on absorbent paper. In the same lard or oil, cook and stir the almonds and pumpkin seeds until they are lightly toasted. In another heavy skillet, without lard or oil, lightly toast the sesame and chili seeds, stirring and watching carefully to see that they do not burn; set aside. Break the bread and tortilla into pieces and place in a blender container. Add the almonds, the pumpkin, sesame and chili seeds, and the onion and garlic. Blend until all ingredients are well ground. Remove this mixture from the blender. Crush the cloves, peppercorn and cinnamon stick in a mortar and add to this mixture; set aside.

Place the drained chilies in the blender container and purée, gradually adding the chicken broth to make a smooth sauce. In a heavy skillet, heat the remaining 2 tablespoons (30 ml) lard or oil, add the crumb-nut-onion mixture and cook and stir for 2 to 3 minutes. Stir in the chili sauce and the shredded chicken. Add salt to taste and cook and stir over medium heat until the mixture has thickened, about 6 minutes. Follow the recipe for Tamales and fill with the chicken filling, then fold and steam as directed.

FISH

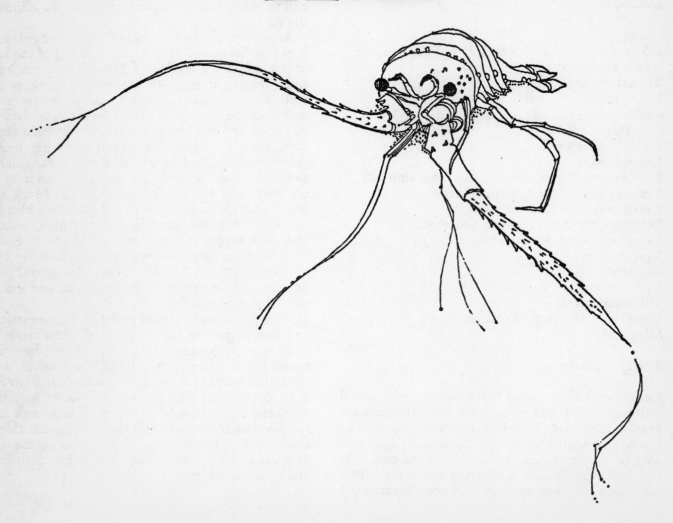

FISH (Pescados)

Mexico is abundant in fish, both from the sea and from fresh water. Among the most interesting of the many fish dishes in the cuisine are the cold dishes, which include Pescado Tricolor, Pescado con Guacamole, Pescado Blanco en Escabeche and Camarones en Frio, as well as Cebiche (see Appetizers).

PESCADO BLANCO DE CHAPALA
White Fish Chapala Style

The great lake of Chapala in the state of Jalisco is a large source of fresh-water fish.

Serves 6
6 small fresh-water fish
Salt
3 eggs, beaten
Olive oil to 1/8 inch (3 mm)
2 pounds (1 kg) tomatoes, roasted
2 *chiles cascabels,* toasted, seeded and deveined
1 medium onion, chopped
2 sprigs cilantro, minced
3 tablespoons (45 ml) white vinegar
3 tablespoons (45 ml) olive oil
Salt to taste

Sprinkle the fish with salt and dip in the beaten eggs. In a heavy skillet, heat the olive oil and fry the fish until golden. Drain on absorbent paper and arrange on a large platter. Purée the tomatoes and chilies together in a blender or food mill, then add the onion, cilantro, vinegar, oil and salt to taste. Pour this sauce over the fish and serve immediately.

PESCADO EN SALSA DE CHILES POBLANOS
Fish in Green Chili Sauce

Fish covered with a wonderful green sauce.

Serves 4
1/2 cup (125 ml) olive oil
1 2-pound (1 kg) fish fillet
10 *chiles poblanos,* roasted, peeled, seeded and deveined
3 garlic cloves, crushed
1 tablespoon (15 ml) minced onion
5 egg yolks
2 cups (500 ml) water
Salt to taste

Brush a small amount of the olive oil over the fish and broil for 5 to 10 minutes, or bake in a preheated 400°F (210°C) oven for 15 to 20 minutes, or until the fish flakes when tested with a fork.

To make the sauce, purée the chilies in a blender or a food mill (if using a blender, add a small amount of water to make a smooth purée). In a heavy skillet, heat the olive oil, add the garlic cloves and cook and stir until golden. Remove the garlic cloves from the pan and add the onion and puréed chilies. Cook and stir over medium heat for several minutes, until slightly thickened; remove from heat and allow to cool slightly. Beat the egg yolks together with the water and mix into the chili-onion mixture. Place over low heat and bring to a simmer, stirring constantly (do not allow the mixture to boil). Continue to stir over low heat until the sauce has thickened. Season with salt to taste. To serve, place the cooked fish on a hot serving platter and pour the sauce over. Serve at once.

PESCADO CON CHILE Y VINO TINTO
Fish with Chili and Red Wine Sauce

Serves 4
2 *chiles anchos,* toasted, seeded and deveined
2 garlic cloves
1 teaspoon (5 ml) cumin seeds
1 *chile poblano,* roasted, peeled, seeded and
  deveined
1-1/2 pounds (750 g) tomatoes, peeled, seeded
  and chopped
1/2 cup (125 ml) olive oil
1 cup (250 ml) red wine
1/2 teaspoon (3 ml) crushed dried oregano
2 tablespoons (30 ml) chopped parsley
1/4 cup (75 ml) pitted green olives, chopped
2 tablespoons (30 ml) capers
Salt and freshly ground black pepper to taste
2 pounds (1 kg) fish fillets, or 4 fish steaks

Soak the *chiles anchos* for 30 minutes in hot water
to cover. Drain the chilies and place them in a
blender container with the garlic cloves; blend to a
purée. Grind the cumin seeds in a spice grinder and
add to the chili purée. Cut the *chile poblano* into
thin strips and set aside. Mix together the chili
purée, chopped tomatoes, oil, wine, oregano, parsley, olives, capers and chili strips; season to taste
with salt and pepper. Lightly grease an ovenproof
baking dish and arrange layers of the fish fillets
alternating with layers of the chili-tomato mixture
(if you are using fish steaks, pour the sauce over).
Place in a preheated 350°F (180°C) oven and bake
until the fish flakes easily with a fork.

PESCADO CON GUACAMOLE
Fish with Guacamole

Serves 6
2 tablespoons (30 ml) lard or corn or safflower oil
1 whole 3-pound (1.5 kg) fish
1 tablespoon (15 ml) oil
1 teaspoon (5 ml) white vinegar
1 recipe Guacamole
1 bunch green onions, trimmed to 6-inch (15 cm)
  lengths
3 to 4 tablespoons (45 to 60 ml) butter
Sliced pimiento-stuffed green olives to taste
Chiles jalapeños in vinegar, drained and minced,
  to taste

In a heavy skillet, heat the lard or oil and cook the
fish on both sides, turning carefully to avoid tear-
ing. When the flesh flakes easily with a fork, remove to a serving platter and let the fish cool.
Carefully remove the skin from the body of the
fish, leaving the head and the tail intact. Mix the
oil and vinegar and spread it over the skinned top
portion of the fish. Place the fish in the refrigerator
to cool for at least one hour.

Just before you are ready to serve, prepare the
guacamole and set aside, covered. In a skillet over
low heat, cook the green onions lightly in the
butter, until the white portion of the onions is just
tender; set aside. Spread the guacamole smoothly
over the skinned portion of the fish and adorn with
the sliced olives and minced chilies in an attractive
pattern (use the olives to simulate fish scales, if
you like). Garnish the platter with the green onions
and serve the fish at once.

PESCADO TRICOLOR
Tricolored Fish

The white, red and green colors of this dish represent the colors of the flag of Mexico. This fish may be served hot or cold.

Serves 6
1 3-pound (1.5 kg) fish fillet
Salt and ground white pepper
2 tablespoons (30 ml) lard or corn or safflower oil
1/2 small onion, minced
1 slice lemon
1 sprig thyme
1 teaspoon (5 ml) white vinegar
1/4 cup (75 ml) water
1 slice good white bread, crust removed
2 tablespoons (30 ml) sesame seeds
2 tablespoons (30 ml) whole blanched almonds
2 tablespoons (30 ml) olive oil
Seeds from 1 small pomegranate, or
   1 red bell pepper, seeded, deveined and minced
1 small bunch watercress

Season the fish with the salt and pepper. In a heavy skillet, heat the lard or oil and cook the fish with the onion, lemon and thyme. Turn the fish once, being careful not to tear it. When the fish flakes easily with a fork, remove it to a platter and keep warm. (If you want to serve this dish cold, allow the fish to cool at this point.)

Mix the vinegar and water and put the slice of bread to soak in it. Toast the sesame seeds lightly by stirring them constantly in a hot, ungreased skillet, taking care not to burn them. Place the soaked bread, with the soaking liquid, in the container of a blender with the sesame seeds and purée the mixture. Add the olive oil and blend to a smooth sauce. Pour this sauce over the warm or cooled fish. Sprinkle pomegranate seeds or minced red bell pepper over, and garnish with sprigs of watercress.

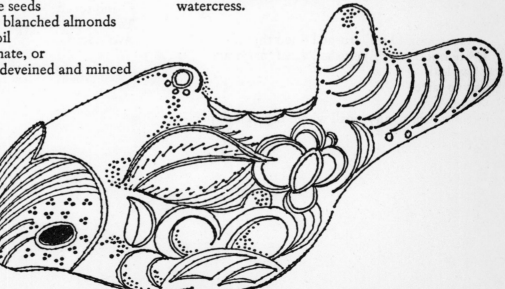

PESCADO BLANCO EN ESCABECHE
Marinated White Fish

In this recipe from Michoacan, the fish is cooked in a poaching liquid, covered with a marinade made of the same ingredients, and served cooled to room temperature or chilled.

Serves 6

Poaching Liquid
4 tablespoons (60 ml) olive oil
3 garlic cloves, crushed
1 medium onion, sliced
3/4 cup (175 ml) white vinegar
2 cups (500 ml) water
1/2 teaspoon (3 ml) sugar
2 peppercorns
2 cloves
1/2 teaspoon (3 ml) crushed dried thyme
1/4 teaspoon (2 ml) crushed dried marjoram
1 bay leaf
Salt to taste

6 white fish, or any small whole fish (1 fish per serving)

Marinade
3/4 cup (175 ml) olive oil
4 tablespoons (60 ml) white vinegar
3 garlic cloves, minced
1 medium onion, sliced
1/2 teaspoon (3 ml) sugar
2 peppercorns
2 cloves
1/2 teaspoon (3 ml) crushed dried thyme
1/4 teaspoon (2 ml) crushed dried marjoram
1 bay leaf
Salt to taste

Shredded romaine lettuce
Green onions sliced lengthwise
Radish roses or slices
Chiles güeros or *jalapeños* in vinegar, drained and sliced
Tomatoes cut in slices or wedges
Avocado slices

To make the poaching liquid, in a Dutch oven or large saucepan heat the oil and cook and stir the garlic and onion until the onion is translucent. Add the remaining ingredients and bring to a boil. Add the fish to the liquid one at a time, cooking them in several batches if necessary so that they are not crowded in the pan. Turn the fish once during the cooking process, about 5 to 10 minutes or until the fish flake when tested with a fork. Remove from the pan, taking care to keep the fish whole, and place them in a shallow casserole.

To make the marinade, mix all the ingredients together in a mixing bowl and pour over the fish. Cool at room temperature for 2 to 3 hours, or chill in the refrigerator for the same amount of time if you want the fish served very cold. Serve on a bed of shredded romaine lettuce on a large platter, surrounded by the onions, radishes, chilies, tomatoes and avocados. Or serve the fish separately, surrounded by bowls of the above ingredients.

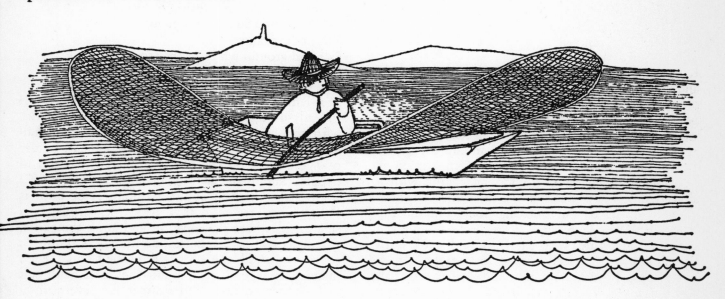

PESCADO NACIONAL
Fried Red Snapper

The red snapper is a very typical Mexican fish, and this is a typical and simple way of preparing it.

Serves 6 to 8
1 3- to 4-pound (1.5 to 2 kg) whole red snapper, or
   3 to 4 pounds (1.5 to 2 kg) red snapper fillets
Salt and ground white pepper to taste
Flour as needed
1/2 cup (125 ml) lard or corn or safflower oil
1 medium onion, chopped
2 garlic cloves, minced

If using a whole fish, wash it well and dry inside and out with absorbent paper. Pat fish fillets dry on all sides with absorbent paper. Sprinkle salt and pepper on all sides of the fish and dust very lightly with flour. In a large skillet, heat the lard or oil almost to the smoking point, then add the onion and garlic and cook and stir until the onion is translucent. Remove the onion and garlic with a slotted spoon and set aside. In the same pan, heat the lard or oil to the smoking point and add the fish. Cook the fish until it is browned on the bottom, then turn very carefully and cook until fish flakes when tested with a fork; remove to a hot platter. Return the onion and garlic to the pan just long enough to heat slightly and serve spooned over the fish.

PÁMPANOS EN SALSA DE AJOS
Pompanos in Garlic Sauce

The pompano is a delicacy of Mexico's coastal waters. This recipe can be made with almost any fish, however, especially red snapper and the various kinds of sole.

Serves 4
6 garlic cloves, minced
6 tablespoons (90 ml) olive oil
1 2-pound (1 kg) pompano, or
   2 1-pound (500 g) pompanos
Juice of 2 oranges
Salt and ground white pepper to taste
2 tablespoons (30 ml) chopped parsley

Mix half of the minced garlic with 3 tablespoons (45 ml) of the olive oil. Coat the fish on all sides with this mixture and allow to marinate in a shallow baking dish at least 1 hour. Pour half of the orange juice over the fish, sprinkle with salt and pepper, and place in a preheated 350°F (180°C) oven. Bake the fish about 20 minutes or until it flakes when tested with a fork. Meanwhile, in a small skillet heat the olive oil and cook the garlic, stirring, for 2 or 3 minutes; do not allow the garlic to brown. Add the chopped parsley and the remaining orange juice. Season the sauce with salt and pepper to taste and simmer for several minutes. Transfer the fish to a serving dish and serve with the hot sauce poured over.

PÁMPANO CAMPECHANO
Pompano Campechan Style

Any small firm-fleshed fish can be substituted for the pompano in this recipe.

Serves 4

1 1-1/2-inch (4 cm) square *achiote* paste, or
    1 tablespoon (15 ml) *achiote* seeds
1 2-pound (1 kg) pompano, or
    2 1-pound (500 g) pompanos
Juice of 3 lemons
Salt to taste
1/2 teaspoon (3 ml) freshly ground black pepper
1/2 teaspoon (3 ml) crushed dried oregano
6 cumin seeds
4 garlic cloves
2 tablespoons (30 ml) olive oil
1 medium onion, sliced
1 lemon, cut in wedges

If using the *achiote* seeds, simmer them in a small amount of water for 10 minutes and allow to soak overnight; set aside. Place the pompano in a shallow baking dish and squeeze the lemon juice over, then sprinkle with salt and allow to marinate for at least 1 hour. Place in a mortar the *achiote* paste or seeds, black pepper, oregano, cumin and garlic. Grind this mixture to a paste, adding water as necessary.

Transfer the marinated pompano to a greased casserole, brushing the fish inside and out with the olive oil and then with the *achiote* mixture. Adorn the fish with overlapping slices of onion and place in a preheated 400°F (210°C) oven. When the fish releases its juices, tilt the pan and remove the juices with a spoon, then return the casserole to the oven until the fish is done, about 15 to 20 minutes in all, or until the fish flakes when tested with a fork. Serve very hot, with wedges of lemon to squeeze over the fish.

HUACHINANGO EN PAPILLOTE A LA CRIOLLA
Red Snapper in Paper, Creole Style

Serves 4
1 pound (500 g) shrimp in their shells
3 tablespoons (45 ml) butter
1/2 teaspoon (3 ml) dry mustard
2 medium onions, minced
1 pound (500 g) tomatoes, peeled, seeded and
    puréed
A pinch of sugar
1 tablespoon (15 ml) whiskey (optional)
1 or 2 *chiles serranos,* seeded, deveined and
    minced
Fresh lime juice to taste
Salt to taste
4 red snapper fillets, about 1/2 pound (250 g)
    each
Butter

Bring a large pot of water to a boil and add the shrimp; cook them for 4 minutes, then remove from the pot, allow to cool, and shell, devein and chop. In a heavy skillet, melt the butter and add the mustard and onions. Cook and stir this mixture for 2 or 3 minutes, then add the shrimp and cook them, stirring, 2 or 3 minutes. Add the tomatoes, sugar, whiskey and chilies and simmer for several minutes. Add the lime juice and salt to taste. Cut 4 pieces of aluminum foil each about 12 inches (30 cm) square. Butter the inside of each square. Cut each fillet in half and place one half in the center of each foil square. Spread one-fourth of the shrimp on this half of fillet, then cover with the other half. Dot with butter. Fold the aluminum foil over the fish, doubling over the edges to seal tightly. Place in a 450°F (230°C) oven for 20 minutes. Serve the fish in its wrapper.

ALBÓNDIGAS DE PESCADO
Fishballs in Tomato Sauce

Serves 6 to 8

Tomato Sauce
4 tablespoons (60 ml) olive oil
1/2 onion, chopped
3 pounds (1.5 kg) tomatoes, peeled, seeded and
  chopped
1 sprig parsley
1 sprig thyme
Salt to taste

Fishballs
3 pounds (1.5 kg) white-fleshed fish fillets
1/4 cup (75 ml) white vinegar
2 slices good white bread, trimmed of crusts
1 tablespoon (15 ml) minced onion
8 ounces (250 g) tomatoes, peeled,
  seeded and minced
1 garlic clove, minced
1 tablespoon (15 ml) minced parsley
3 eggs, beaten
2 *chiles poblanos,* roasted, peeled, seeded,
  deveined and cut into strips
1/2 cup (125 ml) pitted black olives, chopped

To make the tomato sauce, heat the olive oil in a heavy saucepan and add the onion, cooking and stirring until golden. Add the tomatoes, parsley and thyme and cook and stir over medium heat 5 to 10 minutes or until the sauce is slightly thickened; season with salt to taste and keep warm.

To make the fishballs, put the fillets through the fine blade of a meat grinder. Pour the vinegar evenly over the slices of bread to soak them through. Mix the soaked bread with the ground fish, along with the onion, tomato, garlic, parsley and eggs. Form into balls 1-1/2-inches (4 cm) in diameter. Bring the tomato sauce to a simmer and poach the fishballs in the sauce for 15 to 20 minutes. Remove to a heated serving dish with a slotted spoon. Add the chili strips and the olives to the tomato sauce and cook for several minutes; then pour the sauce over the fishballs to serve.

MACUM DE MERO
Halibut Stew

A pungent stew from Yucatán.

Serves 4
1 1-inch (3 cm) square *achiote* paste, or
   1-1/2 teaspoons (8 ml) *achiote* seeds
1 whole head of garlic
20 peppercorns
2 cloves
4 sprigs oregano, or
   1/4 teaspoon (2 ml) crushed dried oregano
1 or 2 *chiles serranos,* seeded, deveined and
   chopped
1/2 cup (125 ml) Seville orange juice, or
   1/4 cup (75 ml) orange juice mixed with
   1/4 cup (75 ml) lemon juice
Salt to taste
2 pounds (1 kg) halibut steaks
4 tablespoons (60 ml) olive oil
1 medium onion, sliced
12 ounces (325 g) tomatoes, sliced
1 green or red bell pepper, seeded,
   deveined and cut into thin strips
2 *chiles güeros*
1 tablespoon (15 ml) minced parsley
1/2 cup (125 ml) water
Olive oil

If you are using the *achiote* seeds, simmer them in a small amount of water for 10 minutes, then soak overnight. Separate the cloves of garlic and toast them, unpeeled, on a heated griddle or in a heated skillet until they are browned; let cool and peel. In a mortar, make a marinade by grinding 4 of the toasted garlic cloves together with the peppercorns, whole cloves, oregano, *achiote* paste or seeds and chilies. Add a few drops of the orange or orange-lemon juice to make a paste, then mix in the rest of the juice and add salt to taste. Place the fish in a shallow pan and pour the marinade over. Marinate for at least 1 hour.

In a Dutch oven or heavy casserole, heat the 4 tablespoons (60 ml) olive oil and cook the remaining garlic cloves until they are golden brown. Remove the garlic from the pan and add half of the onion slices. Place the marinated fish steaks over the onion slices in 1 layer, then cover with the remaining onion slices, the tomato, bell pepper, browned garlic cloves, whole chilies and parsley. Pour over the water and any remaining marinade and sprinkle liberally with olive oil. Cover tightly and cook over low heat for about 30 minutes, or until the fish flakes when tested with a fork and the vegetables are well cooked.

CAMARONES EN FRIO
Cold Marinated Shrimp

Serves 4 to 6
4 large white onions
Juice of one lemon
2 pounds (1 kg) large shrimp
1 cup (250 ml) corn or safflower oil
3 garlic cloves, crushed
1 small can *chiles jalapeños* in vinegar
1/2 cup (125 ml) white vinegar
1/2 teaspoon (3 ml) hot prepared mustard or to
   taste
Reserved juice from the chilies
Salt and ground white pepper to taste
3 large tomatoes, sliced and sprinkled with
Salt and freshly ground black pepper

Slice 3 of the onions, break the slices into rings and squeeze lemon juice over them. Cover and refrigerate for 2 hours. Rinse the shrimp well, and, if you like, shell and devein them (they will retain more flavor if cooked in their shells). Slice the remaining onion. In a heavy skillet, heat one-half of the oil and add the onion and garlic. Cook until the onion is translucent, then add the shrimp and cook until the shrimp turn pink. Discard the garlic, and set the shrimp aside to cool.

Open the can of chilies, being careful to reserve the juice. Seed the chilies and cut them into small strips; set aside. When the shrimp have cooled, cover them with a dressing made of the remaining oil, mixed with the vinegar, hot mustard, reserved juice from the canned chilies and salt and pepper to taste. Garnish the shrimp with the seasoned slices of tomatoes and the chili strips.

CANGREJOS HORNEADOS
Baked Crab

A recipe from Campeche.

Serves 4 to 6
2 live Dungeness crabs
1 red or green bell pepper, roasted, peeled,
  seeded and deveined
12 ounces (325 g) tomatoes, roasted
1 tablespoon (15 ml) lard or corn or safflower oil
1 small onion, minced
3 tablespoons (45 ml) minced pitted green olives
2 tablespoons (30 ml) capers
Salt and ground white pepper to taste
Butter
3 tablespoons (45 ml) bread crumbs
4 tablespoons (60 ml) olive oil

Place the crabs in a large pot of boiling water and cook 2 minutes. Remove the crabs from the pot and place in a steamer to cook (this method will preserve more flavor). As soon as the crabs begin to turn red, remove them from heat and allow them to cool in the steamer. When the crabs are cool, break off the claws and remove the meat from the shell, discarding the spongy material. Crack the claws and remove the meat. Wash the shells thoroughly and set aside.

Mince the bell pepper and, if you like, strain the roasted tomatoes through a sieve or a food mill. In a large, heavy skillet, heat the lard or oil and cook the onion and bell pepper until the onion is translucent, then add the tomatoes, crabmeat, olives and capers. Cook and stir the mixture over low heat until slightly thickened, then add salt and pepper to taste.

Butter the crab shells well and fill with the crab mixture. Dust with bread crumbs and sprinkle with olive oil. Bake in a preheated 375°F (190°C) oven until lightly browned.

OSTIONES ESTOFADOS
Stewed Oysters

Serves 4
4 tablespoons (60 ml) butter
1 onion, minced
3 garlic cloves, minced
1 tablespoon (15 ml) flour
8 ounces (250 g) tomatoes, roasted and strained
2-1/2 dozen fresh oysters
1 cup (250 ml) milk or heavy cream, heated
Salt and ground white pepper to taste
Minced parsley to taste (optional)

In a heavy skillet, heat the butter and cook and stir the onion and garlic until golden. Mix the flour into the tomato purée and add this mixture to the pan; cook over medium heat, stirring constantly until slightly thickened. Add the oysters and simmer until the edges of the oysters curl. Add the heated milk or cream and season to taste with salt and pepper. Simmer a few minutes longer to blend the flavors. Sprinkle with parsley, if you like. Serve very hot.

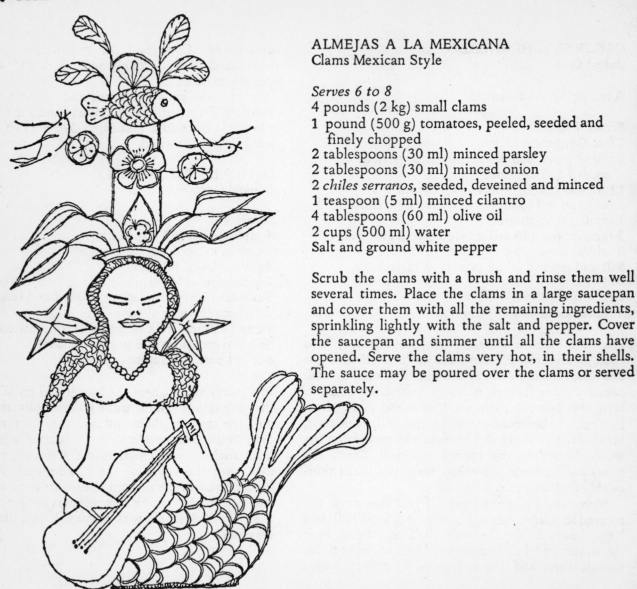

ALMEJAS A LA MEXICANA
Clams Mexican Style

Serves 6 to 8
4 pounds (2 kg) small clams
1 pound (500 g) tomatoes, peeled, seeded and
   finely chopped
2 tablespoons (30 ml) minced parsley
2 tablespoons (30 ml) minced onion
2 *chiles serranos*, seeded, deveined and minced
1 teaspoon (5 ml) minced cilantro
4 tablespoons (60 ml) olive oil
2 cups (500 ml) water
Salt and ground white pepper

Scrub the clams with a brush and rinse them well
several times. Place the clams in a large saucepan
and cover them with all the remaining ingredients,
sprinkling lightly with the salt and pepper. Cover
the saucepan and simmer until all the clams have
opened. Serve the clams very hot, in their shells.
The sauce may be poured over the clams or served
separately.

PULPOS BORRACHOS
Drunken Octopus

Squid may be substituted for octopus in this recipe.

Serves 4
2 pounds (1 kg) octopus or squid
1/2 cup (125 ml) brandy
Salt
1/4 cup (75 ml) olive oil
1 large onion, minced
2 garlic cloves, minced
2 pounds (1 kg) tomatoes, peeled, seeded and
  puréed
2 tablespoons (30 ml) chopped parsley
1 cup (250 ml) red wine
Salt and freshly ground black pepper to taste
Capers to taste
Chopped pitted green olives to taste

Clean the octopus by removing the mouth, eyes, ink sac, ends of the tentacles and cartilage. Wash well. If using squid, peel the tail section and cut out the eye section, ink sac, innards, cartilage and inner bone; wash well. Pound vigorously with a rolling pin to tenderize. Place the octopus or squid in a bowl, pour over the brandy and sprinkle with salt; allow to marinate for 1 hour.

Empty the octopus or squid and the marinade into a large saucepan and add water to cover. Bring to a boil and simmer, covered, until tender (this will take from about 1 to 3 hours, depending on size; octopus will take a longer cooking time than squid). Allow to cool slightly in the cooking broth, then cut in small pieces.

In a large skillet or casserole, heat the olive oil and add the onion and garlic; cook and stir until the onion is translucent. Add the tomatoes and cook over medium heat, stirring occasionally, until the sauce has thickened slightly. Add the parsley, then the octopus or squid along with the cooking broth. Stir in the wine and season to taste with salt and pepper. Simmer, uncovered, until the flavors mingle and the broth is slightly reduced. Just before serving, add capers and chopped olives to taste.

BIRDS

BIRDS *(Aves)*

The turkey and many other game birds are native to Mexico, and poultry dishes are among the most exotic and ancient in the cuisine. The Indian origin of many of the following recipes can be seen in the extensive use of seeds and nuts as sauce ingredients. Most elaborate are the *moles;* because they are both complex and unique they are perfect celebration or feast day dishes.

POLLO A LA MEXICANA
Chicken Mexican Style

Serves 4 to 5
2 *chiles poblanos,* roasted, peeled, seeded and
  deveined
4 tablespoons (60 ml) lard or corn or safflower oil
1 3-1/2-pound (1.75 kg) chicken, cut into serving
  pieces
1 medium onion, thinly sliced
1 pound (500 g) tomatoes, peeled, seeded and
  puréed
1 garlic clove, minced
1 teaspoon (5 ml) salt
1 sprig cilantro
1/2 cup (125 ml) unpitted green olives
Cilantro sprigs (optional)

Cut the chilies into thin strips and set aside. In a heavy skillet, heat the lard or oil almost to the smoking point and brown the chicken on all sides. Remove the chicken from the pan and cook the onion and chili strips in the remaining lard or oil until the onion is translucent. Return the chicken to the pan along with the tomato and garlic. Season with salt and add the cilantro and olives. Cover and simmer until the chicken is tender and the sauce has thickened, 30 to 45 minutes, adding water, if necessary, during the cooking process. Adjust seasoning. Serve garnished with cilantro, if you like.

POLLO JALAPEÑO
Chicken with *Jalapeño* Chilies

A *picante* chicken dish from Veracruz.

Serves 4 to 5
2 pounds (1 kg) tomatoes, roasted
1 small onion, chopped
1 clove garlic
1 tablespoon (15 ml) chopped cilantro
1/4 teaspoon (2 ml) crushed dried oregano
A pinch of ground cloves
1 teaspoon (5 ml) salt
1/8 teaspoon (0.5 ml) freshly ground black pepper
1 tablespoon (15 ml) white vinegar
1 3-1/2-pound (1.75 kg) chicken, cut into serving
  pieces
5 *chiles jalapeños,* seeded, deveined and cut
  into small strips
5 tablespoons (75 ml) olive oil

Purée together in a blender or food mill the tomatoes, onion, garlic, cilantro and oregano. Season with the cloves, salt, pepper and vinegar. Place the chicken in a casserole and cover it with the sauce and the chilies. Sprinkle with the oil and place in a preheated 450°F (230°C) oven. Cook, uncovered, until the chicken is tender and slightly charred and the sauce is absorbed, 45 minutes to 1 hour.

PIPIÁN ROJO DE PEPITA
Chicken in Red Pumpkin Seed Sauce

Duck, turkey or pork can be used in place of chicken in this recipe.

Serves 4 to 6
4 *chiles anchos,* toasted, seeded and deveined
1 3-1/2- to 4-pound (1.75 to 2 kg) chicken,
    cut into serving pieces
4 cups (1 L) chicken broth
1 cup (250 ml) unsalted hulled pumpkin seeds
1 slice good white bread, toasted
4 tablespoons (60 ml) lard or corn or safflower oil
1 sprig thyme
1 teaspoon (5 ml) salt
3 cups (750 ml) reserved chicken broth

Soak the *chiles anchos* in hot water to cover overnight. The next day, place the chicken in a large saucepan, add the broth, bring to a boil and reduce heat. Cover partially and simmer until tender, about 30 to 45 minutes. Allow the chicken to cool in the broth. Toast the pumpkin seeds very lightly by stirring them constantly in a hot, ungreased skillet. Grind the seeds and the toasted bread in a spice grinder or blender. In a heavy skillet, heat 2 tablespoons (30 ml) of the lard or oil and cook the ground seeds 2 or 3 minutes. Drain the chilies and purée in a blender or food mill. In a second heavy skillet, heat the remaining 2 tablespoons (30 ml) lard or oil and cook and stir the purée 2 or 3 minutes. Add the seeds to the purée with the thyme and salt; stir in the reserved chicken broth. Place the pieces of cooked chicken in the sauce and cook over low heat 15 or 20 minutes, or until the sauce has thickened. Adjust seasoning and serve.

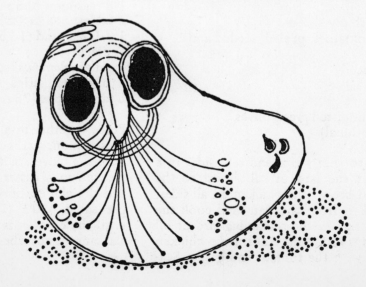

PIPIÁN VERDE DE PEPITA
Chicken in Green Pumpkin Seed Sauce

Duck, turkey or pork can also be used for this dish, and slices of chayote can be used in place of the lettuce.

Serves 4 to 6
1 3-1/2- to 4-pound (1.75 to 2 kg) chicken,
    cut into serving pieces
2 garlic cloves
4 cups (1 L) chicken broth
1 cup (250 ml) unsalted hulled pumpkin seeds
3 peppercorns
A pinch of aniseed
2 pounds (1 kg) *tomatillos,* husked, or
    4 cups (1 L) canned *tomatillos,* drained
1 onion, chopped
3 or 4 *chiles serranos,* seeded and deveined
1 large romaine lettuce leaf
2 cups (500 ml) reserved chicken broth
4 tablespoons (60 ml) lard or corn or safflower oil
1 teaspoon (5 ml) salt

Place the chicken in a large saucepan, add the garlic and chicken broth and bring to a boil. Reduce heat, cover partially, and simmer until tender, about 30 to 45 minutes. Allow the chicken to cool in the broth. Toast the pumpkin seeds very lightly by stirring them in a hot, ungreased frying pan. Grind the toasted pumpkin seeds, together with the peppercorns and aniseed, in a spice grinder or blender. If you are using fresh *tomatillos,* place them in a saucepan with salted water to cover, bring to a boil, reduce heat and simmer until tender, about 10 minutes. Purée the *tomatillos,* onion, chilies and lettuce in a blender, then add the seed-spice mixture and enough of the reserved broth to make a smooth sauce. In a heavy skillet, heat the lard or oil and cook the sauce over high heat for 3 or 4 minutes, stirring constantly. Reduce heat, stir in the remaining broth and season with salt, then add the chicken. Be careful not to stir the sauce after this point, as it can separate. Simmer gently until the chicken is heated through.

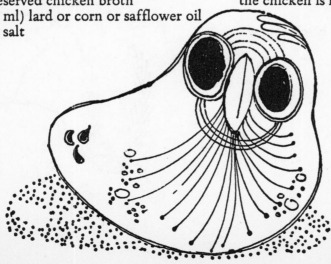

POLLO EN CEBOLLA
Chicken with Onions

A recipe from Puebla. It may seem to you that you are using an enormous amount of nutmeg, but the long, slow cooking process blends all the flavors of this dish together to make a rich, savory sauce. New peas cooked in butter are a good choice for an accompanying vegetable. This dish is also very good reheated.

Serves 4 to 5
4 tablespoons (60 ml) lard or corn or safflower oil
1 3-1/2-pound (1.75 kg) chicken, cut into
    serving pieces
3 large onions, chopped
1 garlic clove
2 or 3 cups (500 or 750 ml) water
1 teaspoon (5 ml) crushed dried thyme
1 bay leaf
1 sprig cilantro
1 teaspoon (5 ml) salt
1/8 teaspoon (0.5 ml) freshly ground black pepper
1 whole nutmeg
Sprigs of cilantro (optional)

In a heavy skillet, heat the lard or oil almost to the smoking point and brown the chicken on all sides. Remove from the pan. In the same lard or oil, cook the onions and garlic over low heat, stirring frequently, until they turn a deep golden brown (this could take 20 to 30 minutes). Return the chicken to the pan and add the water, thyme, bay leaf, cilantro, salt and pepper. Grate the whole nutmeg over the chicken. Cover the pan and simmer about 1-1/2 hours, or until the chicken is very tender and the sauce is dark and thick. Garnish with cilantro, if you like.

PIPIÁN VERDE DE AJONJOLÍ
Chicken in Green Sesame Sauce

This dish can also be made with country-style pork spareribs.

Serves 4 to 5
1 4-pound (2 kg) chicken,
   cut into serving pieces
4 cups (1 L) chicken broth
1 cup (250 ml) sesame seeds
4 tablespoons (60 ml) lard or corn or safflower oil
2 pounds (1 kg) *tomatillos*, husked, or
   4 cups (1 L) canned *tomatillos*, drained
1 onion, quartered
3 to 4 *chiles serranos*, seeded and deveined
1 garlic clove
4 romaine lettuce leaves
1 sprig cilantro
1 sprig *epazote* (optional)
2 cups (500 ml) reserved chicken broth
Salt to taste

Place the chicken in a large saucepan, add the broth, bring to a boil and reduce heat. Cover partially and simmer until tender, about 30 to 45 minutes. Allow the chicken to cool in the broth. Toast the sesame seeds in a hot, ungreased frying pan, stirring constantly and taking care not to burn them. Grind the seeds in a spice grinder or blender. In a heavy skillet, heat 2 tablespoons (30 ml) of the lard or oil and fry the ground seeds 2 or 3 minutes, stirring constantly. Place the *tomatillos*, onion and chilies in a saucepan, cover with water, bring to a boil and simmer, covered, for 10 minutes; drain. (If using canned *tomatillos*, cook the onion and chilies together, drain, and purée in a blender or food mill with the drained *tomatillos*.) Purée the vegetables in a blender or food mill together with the garlic, lettuce, cilantro and *epazote* sprigs. In a heavy skillet, heat the remaining 2 tablespoons (30 ml) lard or oil and fry the sauce over medium heat for 5 minutes, stirring constantly. Add the reserved broth and season to taste with salt. Add the chicken and simmer until the sauce has thickened, about 10 minutes.

POLLO MARISCALA
Marshal's Wife's Chicken

Chicken in a chicken-liver sauce—a dish from Vera-cruz.

Serves 4
2 tablespoons (30 ml) lard or corn or
    safflower oil
16 chicken livers
1 garlic clove, minced
1 small onion, minced
3 hard-cooked egg yolks
2 tablespoons (30 ml) minced parsley
1/2 cup (125 ml) hot beef broth or more
Salt to taste
Freshly ground black pepper to taste
White vinegar to taste
2 tablespoons (30 ml) olive oil
4 chicken breasts, skinned and boned
Chopped romaine lettuce leaves
Sprigs of cilantro

In a heavy skillet, heat the lard or oil and cook the chicken livers, garlic and 1 tablespoon (15 ml) of the minced onion until the livers are browned but still slightly pink inside. Set aside 4 of the livers. Place the remaining livers, egg yolks and parsley in a blender and purée, adding the beef broth to make a smooth sauce. Pour into a saucepan, add salt, pepper and vinegar and simmer until slightly thickened. In a heavy skillet, heat the olive oil and add the remaining minced onion; cook and stir until the onion is translucent. Add the chicken breasts to the skillet and cook over low heat until the chicken is just cooked through; the chicken should not brown. Pour the sauce over the chicken and simmer a few minutes longer. Serve at once on a platter garnished with lettuce and cilantro.

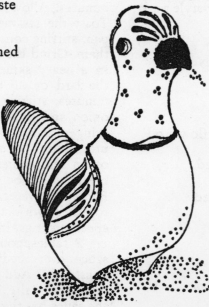

GALLINA EN MOLE SABROSA
Chicken in Savory Sauce

Duck can be used in place of chicken in this recipe.

Serves 4
3/4 cup (175 ml) lard or corn or safflower oil
1 4-pound (2 kg) roasting chicken, cut into quarters
5 *chiles anchos,* seeded and deveined
5 *chiles chipotles,* seeded and deveined
1/2 cup (125 ml) golden raisins
1/2 cup (125 ml) slivered blanched almonds
1 slice good white bread, crust removed
1/2 cup (125 ml) white vinegar
1/2 cinnamon stick
1 clove
3 peppercorns
1/2 teaspoon (3 ml) crushed dried oregano
1 cup (250 ml) fresh orange juice
1 tablespoon (15 ml) sugar
Salt to taste

In a heavy skillet, heat 4 tablespoons (60 ml) of the lard or oil and brown the chicken well on all sides. Cover and simmer, with just enough water to keep from sticking, until tender, about 45 minutes. While the chicken is cooking, heat 4 tablespoons (60 ml) of the lard or oil in another skillet and fry the chilies until soft; drain on absorbent paper. In the same skillet, fry the raisins until plump, remove and drain, then fry the almonds until lightly browned, remove and drain. Lastly, fry the bread until lightly browned, then remove and drain. Purée all of these ingredients together in a blender, adding the white vinegar to make a smooth sauce. Grind the cinnamon, clove, peppercorns and oregano together in a spice grinder or mortar and add to the chili mixture. In the same skillet, heat the remaining 4 tablespoons (60 ml) lard or oil and cook the sauce over high heat for 4 or 5 minutes, stirring constantly. Add the orange juice and sugar and season to taste with salt. Add the cooked chicken to the sauce and simmer 15 to 20 minutes, until the sauce has thickened.

PIPIÁN COLORADO DE AJONJOLÍ
Chicken in Red Sesame Sauce

Country-style pork spareribs can be substituted for the chicken in this recipe.

Serves 4 to 6
6 *chiles anchos*
6 tablespoons (90 ml) lard or corn or safflower oil
1/2 teaspoon (3 ml) salt
A squirt of vinegar
1 3-1/2- to 4-pound (1.75 to 2 kg) chicken,
   cut into serving pieces
4 cups (1 L) chicken broth
1 pound (500 g) tomatoes, roasted
1 onion, chopped
2 garlic cloves, toasted
1 cup (250 ml) sesame seeds
1 tablespoon (15 ml) reserved chili seeds, or to taste
8 cloves
1/2 cinnamon stick
Salt to taste

Cut open the chilies and remove the veins and seeds, reserving the seeds. In a heavy skillet, heat 2 tablespoons (30 ml) of the lard or oil and fry the chilies lightly. Remove from the pan and soak them overnight in boiling water to cover, adding the salt and vinegar.

The next day, place the chicken in a large saucepan, add the broth, bring to a boil and reduce to a simmer. Partially cover and cook until tender, about 30 to 45 minutes. Set the chicken aside to cool in the broth, then drain, reserving the broth.

Drain the soaked chilies and purée them in a blender or food mill together with the tomatoes, onion and garlic. Toast the sesame seeds and reserved chili seeds very lightly in a hot, ungreased frying pan, stirring constantly and taking care not to burn them. Grind the seed mixture along with the cloves and cinnamon stick in a spice grinder or blender. Heat the remaining 4 tablespoons (60 ml) lard or oil and fry the ground seeds lightly, stirring constantly, until the mixture begins to form a mass. Add the puréed tomato-chili mixture and fry over medium heat for 3 or 4 minutes. Add the reserved broth and boil the sauce until it has thickened slightly. Add the chicken, the ground spices and salt to taste. Cook over low heat until the chicken is heated through.

POLLITOS EN VINO TINTO
Little Chickens in Red Wine

Serves 6
1/2 cup (125 ml) olive oil
1/2 cup (125 ml) white vinegar
1 medium onion, sliced
2 garlic cloves, crushed
1 bay leaf
1 sprig thyme
1 teaspoon (5 ml) salt
1/8 teaspoon (0.5 ml) freshly ground black pepper
2 2-1/2-pound (1.25 kg) chickens, cut into
   serving pieces
4 slices bacon
1-1/2 pounds (750 g) tomatoes, peeled, seeded
   and chopped
2 carrots, chopped
6 whole green onions, chopped in 1-inch (3 cm)
   pieces
2 cups (500 ml) dry red wine

Combine the oil, vinegar, onion, garlic, bay leaf, thyme, salt and pepper and marinate the chicken in this mixture for 24 hours. Cut the bacon into squares and fry it lightly in a heavy skillet until all the fat has been rendered out. Add the tomatoes, carrots and green onions to the bacon and its fat and cook over medium heat for 5 minutes, then add the chicken with the marinade. Add the wine, bring to a boil and reduce to a simmer. Cover and cook until tender, about 1 hour.

MANCHAMANTELES
"Tablecloth Stainer"

A traditional Mexican dish, this is an exuberant combination of chicken and pork, vegetables and fruit in a red chili sauce that gives the stew its name.

Serves 8 to 10
8 *chiles pasillas* or *anchos*
A pinch of salt
1 teaspoon (5 ml) white vinegar
1 4-pound (2 kg) chicken, cut into serving pieces
1 pound (500 g) country-style pork spareribs,
    cut into serving pieces
1 large sweet potato or yam
5 tablespoons (75 ml) lard or corn or safflower oil
1 slice good white bread, crust removed
2 garlic cloves
1 medium onion, chopped
1 tablespoon (15 ml) peeled peanuts
1-1/2 pounds (750 g) tomatoes, peeled, seeded
    and chopped
3 cups (750 ml) reserved chicken broth
3 cups (750 ml) reserved pork broth
1 tablespoon (15 ml) sugar
1 tablespoon (15 ml) white vinegar
Salt to taste
8 ounces (250 g) peas, shelled
3 medium apples, peeled, cored and sliced
2 slices fresh pineapple, cut in chunks
1 very ripe plantain or 1 firm banana

Soak the chilies overnight in hot water to cover, along with the salt and vinegar. The next day remove the chilies from the soaking water and drain; set aside. Place the chicken, pork and sweet potato or yam in separate saucepans with salted water to cover, cover each partially, bring to a boil, then reduce heat and simmer until tender, about 45 minutes for the chicken and pork and 20 minutes for the sweet potato or yam. Drain the sweet potato or yam and set aside. Allow the chicken and pork to cool in their broth, then drain, reserving the broth.

To prepare the chili sauce, in a small skillet heat 1 tablespoon (15 ml) of the lard or oil almost to the smoking point and fry the slice of bread until golden. Place the bread in a blender container along with the chilies, garlic, onion, peanuts and tomatoes and purée (add reserved broth as necessary to make a smooth purée). In a large skillet, heat the remaining 4 tablespoons (60 ml) lard or oil and cook and stir the purée over medium heat for 2 to 3 minutes, then add the reserved chicken and pork broth and simmer about 10 minutes longer. Stir in the sugar and vinegar and season to taste with salt.

Place the chicken and pork in a large pot and add the chili sauce. Add the peas and apples. Peel the sweet potato or yam, cut into thick slices and add to the stew along with the pineapple. Simmer about 10 minutes longer and adjust the seasoning. Peel and slice the plantain or banana in crosswise slices, add to the stew and serve in large soup bowls.

CODORNICES
Braised Quail

A recipe from San Luis Potosí.

Serves 6
6 quail
1 cup (250 ml) corn or safflower oil
1/2 cup (125 ml) white vinegar
12 ounces (325 g) tomatoes, chopped
1 medium onion, chopped
3 garlic cloves, crushed
1/2 teaspoon (3 ml) each crushed dried thyme
    and marjoram
1/2 teaspoon (3 ml) freshly ground black pepper
1/2 teaspoon (3 ml) salt
6 *chiles jalapeños* in vinegar, drained, seeded
    and halved

Marinate the quail overnight in a mixture of the
oil, vinegar, tomatoes, onion, garlic, herbs and
spices. The next day, cook with the marinade in a
covered pan over a slow fire until tender, about 30
minutes or more. To serve, garnish with the *jalapeño* chilies.

MOLE POBLANO
Turkey in *Mole* Sauce, Pueblan Style

This *mole* from Puebla is the famous sauce containing chocolate; once cooked, the chocolate blends with all the other ingredients to make a dark, delicious sauce.

Serves 10 to 12
1 7- to 8-pound (3.5 to 4 kg) turkey
3/4 cup (175 ml) lard or corn or safflower oil
3 *chiles chipotles,* seeded and deveined
2 pounds (1 kg) tomatoes, roasted
3 quarts (3 L) chicken broth
1 teaspoon (5 ml) salt
8 *chiles mulatos*
6 *chiles anchos*
4 *chiles pasillas*
1 teaspoon (5 ml) aniseed
3/4 cup (175 ml) sesame seeds
1/2 cup (125 ml) slivered blanched almonds
1/4 cup (75 ml) peeled peanuts
1/4 cup (75 ml) golden raisins
1 slice good white bread
1 corn tortilla
2 large onions, chopped
6 garlic cloves
10 peppercorns
4 cloves
1 cinnamon stick
2 ounces (50 g) Mexican chocolate

Cut the turkey into serving pieces. In a large, heavy skillet or Dutch oven, heat 6 tablespoons (90 ml) of the lard or oil and brown the turkey well on all sides; set aside. Boil the *chiles chipotles* in water for 5 minutes, drain and purée in a blender or food mill with the roasted tomatoes. Add this sauce to the browned turkey and simmer, uncovered, until all the liquid has evaporated. Add 1 quart (1 L) of the chicken broth to the turkey, season with salt, and cover and cook until the turkey is tender, about 45 minutes to 1 hour.

Seed and devein the *chiles mulatos, anchos* and *pasillas.* In a heavy skillet, heat 3 tablespoons (45 ml) lard or oil and fry the chilies lightly, then drain on absorbent paper and purée in a blender or food mill; set aside. Toast the aniseed and sesame seeds lightly by stirring them constantly in an ungreased frying pan; set aside. In the same skillet used to fry the chilies, heat the remaining 3 tablespoons (45 ml) lard or oil and fry the following ingredients separately, draining each on absorbent paper after frying and then placing in a blender container: almonds, peanuts, raisins, white bread and tortilla (break the last two in pieces before adding to the blender). Add the fried chilies, 1/2 cup (125 ml) of the sesame seeds, the aniseed, onions and garlic to the blender jar and purée, adding enough of the chicken broth to make a smooth sauce. Pour the sauce into a large flame-proof casserole and stir in the remaining chicken broth. Add the chocolate and stir over low heat until melted. Grind the spices in a mortar or spice grinder; add to sauce. Add turkey and simmer about 15 minutes or until the flavors have blended. Sprinkle with the remaining sesame seeds and serve.

MOLE DE PAVO
Turkey in a *Mole* Sauce

A *mole* without chocolate, and with *tomatillos*.

Serves 10 to 12
12 *chiles anchos*
3 *chiles pasillas*
3 *chiles mulatos*
2 tablespoons (30 ml) lard or corn or safflower oil
A pinch of salt
1 tablespoon (15 ml) white vinegar
1 7- to 8-pound (3.5 to 4 kg) turkey
3/4 cup (175 ml) lard or corn or safflower oil
The turkey neck and giblets
8 ounces (250 g) *tomatillos*, husked, or
   1 cup (250 ml) canned *tomatillos*, drained
1/4 cup (75 ml) unblanched almonds
1/4 cup (75 ml) golden raisins
2 tablespoons (30 ml) sesame seeds
2 tablespoons (30 ml) coriander seeds
2 corn tortillas
1/2 teaspoon (3 ml) each ground cloves, cinnamon
   and black pepper
Reserved turkey broth as needed
Salt to taste
1 bay leaf

The night before you plan to serve this dish, seed and devein the chilies, then heat the lard or oil in a heavy skillet and fry the chilies just until soft. Drain and cover with hot water, add the salt and vinegar and soak overnight. (Rinse after 30 minutes and add fresh hot water, vinegar and salt if you want the sauce to be mild.) Next day, drain the chilies, reserving the soaking water, and blend them in a blender with just enough of their soaking water to make a coarse sauce; set aside.

Cut the turkey into serving pieces. In a large, heavy skillet, heat 6 tablespoons (90 ml) of the lard or oil and brown the turkey well on all sides. Cover and cook over low heat until tender (adding water if necessary) about 45 minutes to 1 hour. While the turkey is cooking, place the turkey neck and the giblets in a saucepan with salted water to cover, bring to a boil, then reduce heat and simmer, covered, for about 30 minutes to make a rich broth; set aside.

If you are using fresh *tomatillos*, place them in salted water to cover, bring to a boil, then reduce heat and simmer until tender, about 10 minutes; drain and set aside. In a heavy skillet, heat 4 tablespoons (60 ml) of the lard or oil and lightly fry each of the following ingredients separately, drain on absorbent paper and place in a blender jar: almonds, raisins, sesame seeds, coriander seeds, tortillas (broken into pieces) and *tomatillos*. Add the ground cloves, cinnamon and pepper to the blender jar and blend all the ingredients together. Add this mixture to the puréed chilies, mixing in just enough reserved broth from the neck and giblets to make a smooth sauce. In the same skillet used to fry the preceding ingredients, heat the remaining 2 tablespoons (30 ml) lard or oil and fry the sauce 5 minutes over medium heat, stirring constantly. Season with salt to taste. When the turkey is tender, add the turkey and the bay leaf to the sauce and simmer 15 to 20 minutes. Remove the bay leaf before serving.

PAVO EN FRIO
Cold Spiced Turkey

A fragrant dish from Yucatán. Duck is also delicious cooked in this manner.

Serves 10 to 12
1 7- to 8-pound (3.5 to 4 kg) turkey
Salt
6 peppercorns, ground
2 ounces (50 g) Canadian bacon, cut into strips
3 garlic cloves, minced
2 avocado leaves, lightly toasted and crumbled
Ground cloves, cinnamon and nutmeg to taste
2 cups (500 ml) chicken broth
1 cup (250 ml) dry white wine
2 oranges, preferably Seville
2 white onions, cut in wedges
1 bay leaf
1/2 teaspoon (3 ml) crushed dried thyme
Salt and ground white pepper to taste
Unpitted green or black olives
Capers
Olive oil to taste
White vinegar to taste

Dry the turkey well inside and out with absorbent paper. Sprinkle the inside of the turkey with salt and pepper; stuff with bacon, garlic and leaves. Sprinkle the outside of the turkey generously with the ground spices, and wrap it tightly in a large square of cheesecloth or muslin, tying the cloth closed with white cotton string. Place the turkey in a pot with the chicken broth and cover tightly; simmer the turkey for 1 to 1-1/2 hours, or until tender. Remove from the pot and unwrap, then return to the pot, adding the wine. With a sharp knife, cut the peel from the oranges down to the flesh, then cut out the sections, leaving the white dividing membrane. Add the orange sections, onions, bay leaf, thyme and salt and pepper to the pot, cover and cook over low heat a few minutes, or until the onions are just partly cooked through. Remove the cover and allow the turkey to cool to room temperature, then remove from the pot, cut into serving pieces and place on a serving platter. Adorn the turkey with the olives and capers and pass the sauce separately, along with oil and vinegar to add to the turkey to taste.

MEATS

MEATS *(Carnes)*

The pig, sheep and cow were brought to Mexico by the Spanish and were soon assimilated into the country's cuisine, cooked with sauces made of chilies, tomatoes, nuts and seeds, and used in tortilla dishes. Pork lard became a basic ingredient of Mexican dishes, and pork, lamb and beef cooked in the Indian *barbacoa* created a new field of cookery, reflected here in the recipes for Lomo de Cerdo Adobado, Cochinita Pibil and Pierna de Carnero Enchilada.

Note: the four *pipiáns* in the Birds section—Verde de Pipita, Rojo de Pepita, Verde de Ajonjolí and Colorado de Ajonjolí—can be prepared with pork in place of chicken.

BISTEQUES CON CHIPOTLE
Steak with *Chipotle* Chilies

Serves 4 to 6
8 ounces (250 g) tomatoes, peeled and seeded
2 *chiles chipotles* in vinegar, drained
3 tablespoons (45 ml) lard or corn or safflower oil
2 pounds (1 kg) sirloin steak
1 large onion, thinly sliced
Salt to taste

Purée the tomatoes and the chilies together in a blender or food mill; set aside. In a heavy skillet, heat the lard or oil to the smoking point; add the steak, then the onion slices. Cook for about 5 minutes on one side, then turn the steak over, add the tomato-chili sauce, and cook about 5 more minutes, or until done to your taste. Season to taste with salt and serve immediately.

CARNE EN TODO JUNTO
Meat with Everything

Serves 6 to 8
2 pounds (1 kg) stewing beef, cut into 2-inch (5 cm) cubes
8 ounces (250 g) tomatoes, peeled, seeded and chopped
1 medium onion, chopped
2 garlic cloves, minced
1 *chile jalapeño*, seeded and minced
1/2 cup (125 ml) lard
1/2 cup (125 ml) white vinegar
1 tablespoon (15 ml) capers
2 tablespoons (30 ml) chopped pitted green olives
5 peppercorns, crushed
1/2 cinnamon stick, ground
A pinch of powdered cloves
1/2 cup (125 ml) slivered blanched almonds
1 bay leaf
1 pinch each dried thyme, marjoram and oregano
Salt to taste

Place the beef in a saucepan and add water to half cover the meat. Add all the remaining ingredients except the salt, and cook over a medium flame, uncovered, 1 hour or more or until the liquid has evaporated and the meat is tender but not falling apart. Add salt to taste. Serve wrapped in hot tortillas.

ALBÓNDIGAS
Meatballs

Serves 6 to 8

Sauce
1-1/2 pounds (750 g) tomatoes, peeled and seeded
1 *chile ancho,* toasted, seeded and deveined, or
   1 *chile chipotle* in vinegar, drained
2 tablespoons (30 ml) lard or corn or safflower oil
1 tablespoon (15 ml) minced onion
1 garlic clove, minced
About 2 cups (500 ml) beef broth or water
Salt to taste

Meatballs
1 pound (500 g) ground sirloin
1 pound (500 g) ground pork
1/4 cup (75 ml) bread crumbs
1/4 cup (75 ml) milk
1 egg, beaten
1 teaspoon (5 ml) crushed dried thyme
1/4 cup (75 ml) minced parsley
1 teaspoon (5 ml) salt
1 jar pitted green or black olives (optional)

To make the sauce, purée the tomatoes and chili in a blender. In a heavy skillet, heat the lard or oil and cook and stir the onion and garlic until the onion is translucent. Pour in the tomato purée and cook and stir over medium heat 3 to 4 minutes. Stir in broth or water to make a thin sauce and season to taste with salt. Transfer to a large saucepan and place over low heat.

To make the meatballs, mix together the ground sirloin and pork. Soak the bread crumbs in the milk for 5 minutes, then stir into the meat mixture. Mix in the egg, thyme, parsley and salt. Form into balls, tucking an olive into the center of each, if you like. Drop the meatballs into the simmering sauce and cover and simmer until cooked through, about 30 minutes.

EMPANADAS DE SANTA RITA
Meat Turnovers

Savory fried meat pies from the state of Chihuahua.

Makes 12

Filling
1 pound (500 g) ground beef
2 potatoes, cooked, peeled and cut in small cubes
1/2 cup (125 ml) cooked green peas
1 tablespoon (15 ml) minced onion
1/2 cup (125 ml) raisins, chopped
A pinch of ground cinnamon
A pinch of ground cloves
Salt and freshly ground black pepper to taste
1/2 cup (125 ml) Madeira or sweet sherry

Pastry
2 cups (475 ml) all-purpose flour
1 teaspoon (5 ml) baking powder
1/2 teaspoon (3 ml) salt
2 tablespoons (30 ml) lard or vegetable shortening
About 1/2 cup (125 ml) ice water

Melted lard or corn or safflower oil to
   1/4 inch (6 mm)

To make the filling, cook and stir the meat in a heavy skillet until browned; drain off fat. Stir in the potatoes, peas, onion and raisins. Season with the spices, then add the wine and cook over medium heat for 4 to 5 minutes, or until the wine is reduced and the meat mixture is almost dry.

To make the pastry, sift the flour, baking powder and salt together. Cut the lard or shortening into the dry ingredients with a pastry cutter or work it in with your fingers. Add enough ice water to form a smooth ball of dough, then roll the dough out on a floured board. Cut in 12 circles 3 or 4 inches (8 or 10 cm) in diameter. Put a spoonful of filling on one half of each circle, wet the edges with water, fold over and press edges firmly together with the tines of a fork.

Allow the filled turnovers to dry for 1 hour, turning them once halfway through the time period. Heat the lard or oil in a heavy skillet and fry the turnovers, turning them to brown on both sides. Drain on absorbent paper. Sprinkle lightly with sugar while they are still hot, if you like.

MOLE DE OLLA
Beef Stew in a Pot

This stew is traditionally cooked in an earthenware pot called an *olla;* a bean pot makes a good substitute, but you can use any large saucepan or a Dutch oven.

Serves 4
1 pound (500 g) stewing beef, cut into
   1-1/2-inch (4 cm) squares
1 onion, chopped
2 garlic cloves, crushed
6 cups (1.5 L) water
3 to 4 *chiles anchos,* toasted, seeded and deveined
12 *chiles cascabels,* toasted, seeded and deveined
1 *tomatillo* (optional)
1 sprig *epazote* (optional)
4 tablespoons (60 ml) lard or corn or safflower oil
4 small zucchini, sliced
2 whole ears of corn, sliced crosswise
Salt to taste
1 lime or lemon, cut in wedges

Place the meat in an earthenware pot, saucepan or Dutch oven, along with the onion and garlic. Add the water and bring to a boil, then partially cover and reduce to a simmer. Cook until the meat is tender, 1-1/2 hours or more. Meanwhile, soak the chilies in hot water to cover for 30 minutes, then purée in a blender or food mill along with the *tomatillo* and *epazote.* In a heavy skillet, heat the lard or oil and cook and stir the purée for 5 to 8 minutes. When the beef is tender, add the chili purée, zucchini and sliced corn to the stew, then cover and simmer until the vegetables are tender, about 20 minutes. Season with salt to taste. Serve from the earthenware pot or a soup tureen, and pass lime or lemon wedges to squeeze over the stew.

MENUDO CON CHORIZO
Tripe with Sausage

Menudo is the traditional dish for New Year's Day. This version calls for the addition of *chorizo* sausage and ham.

Serves 6
2 pounds (1 kg) blanched and parboiled
   honeycomb tripe*
3 tablespoons (45 ml) lard or corn or safflower oil
2 garlic cloves
2 slices good white bread, crusts removed
1 small cinnamon stick
4 peppercorns
1 tablespoon (15 ml) minced onion
1 pound (500 g) tomatoes, peeled and chopped
4 ounces (125 g) ham, chopped
2 *chorizo* sausages, sliced
1 tablespoon (15 ml) chopped parsley
1 sprig thyme
About 1 cup (250 ml) of broth from the tripe
Salt to taste
1 tablespoon (15 ml) olive oil
Chopped pitted green olives
Salsa de Chile Pasilla (optional)

Wash the tripe and cut it into 2-inch (5 cm) squares. Place in a large saucepan, add salted water to cover and bring to a boil. Reduce heat to a simmer, cover pan and allow tripe to cook about 2-1/2 hours, or until tender.

In a heavy skillet, heat the lard or oil almost to the smoking point and lightly fry the garlic and the bread slices. Drain on absorbent paper. Grind the garlic and bread together in a blender. Grind the cinnamon and peppercorns in a mortar or spice grinder and add to the blender; set aside. In the lard or oil remaining in the skillet, cook the onion, tomato, ham and *chorizo* together for 3 to 4 minutes. Add the bread crumb mixture, parsley, thyme and cooked tripe. Add enough tripe broth to make the dish slightly soupy. Season to taste with salt and simmer for about 10 minutes to blend the flavors. To serve, sprinkle with olive oil and chopped olives, and accompany with a bowl of Salsa de Chile Pasilla if you want the *menudo* to be *picante*.

*Tripe is usually purchased already blanched, parboiled and cut into sections.

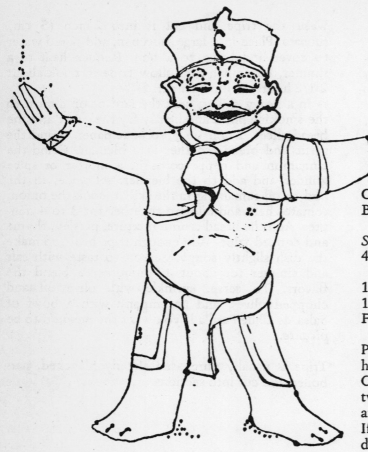

CARNITAS
Browned Pork Bits

Serves 8 to 10
4-1/2 pounds (2.25 kg) pork butt or
    shoulder, cut into 1-inch (3 cm) cubes
1 small onion, chopped
1 teaspoon (5 ml) salt
Freshly ground black pepper

Place the meat in a pot with salted water to half cover the meat. Add all remaining ingredients. Cook uncovered over a medium flame for up to two hours, or until all the liquid has evaporated and the *carnitas* have browned in their own fat. If the liquid evaporates before the meat is tender, add a little more. Adjust seasoning before serving. Serve wrapped in hot tortillas.

Note You may want to trim the meat of excess fat and pour off any excess fat at the end of the cooking time, but some fat is necessary in order to brown the meat.

LOMO DE CERDO EN CHILE VERDE
Pork Loin in Green Chili Sauce

Serves 4
2 tablespoons (30 ml) olive oil
2 pounds (1 kg) pork loin, cut into chops
2 pounds (1 kg) *tomatillos,* husked or
    4 cups (1 L) canned *tomatillos,* drained
1 small onion, chopped
1 romaine lettuce leaf, chopped
1 garlic clove
1 sprig cilantro
2 *chiles poblanos,* roasted, peeled, seeded,
    deveined and chopped
1 teaspoon (5 ml) salt
Freshly ground black pepper to taste
1/4 cup (75 ml) water

In a heavy skillet, heat the oil and brown the chops. Remove the chops from the pan, reserving the cooking oil remaining in the pan. If you are using fresh *tomatillos,* cook them in boiling salted water to cover until tender, about 10 minutes. Purée together in a blender the *tomatillos,* onion, lettuce leaf, garlic, cilantro and chilies, adding a small amount of water, if necessary, to make a smooth purée. Heat the reserved cooking oil in the pan used to brown the chops, add the sauce and cook and stir over medium heat for 3 to 4 minutes. Add salt and pepper, then add the chops and the water. Cover and simmer over low heat about 30 minutes, or until the chops are tender and the sauce is slightly thickened. Adjust seasoning and serve.

LOMO DE CERDO EN NARANJA
Pork Loin in Orange Sauce

Serves 6 to 8
3 pounds (1.5 kg) boneless pork loin
1 tablespoon (15 ml) ground cinnamon
1/4 teaspoon (1 ml) ground cloves
Salt and freshly ground black pepper
3 tablespoons (45 ml) corn or safflower oil
1 medium onion, chopped
2 garlic cloves
1 cup (250 ml) fresh orange juice or more
1 cup (250 ml) hot water or more
1/4 cup (75 ml) golden raisins
2 tablespoons (30 ml) capers
1/4 cup (75 ml) slivered blanched almonds
2 oranges, peeled, sliced and seeded

Sprinkle the pork with the cinnamon, cloves and salt and pepper. Heat the oil and brown the meat on all sides, adding the onion and garlic toward the end of the cooking time. When the onion is tender, pour in the orange juice and water. Cover and cook over low heat until the meat is tender, about 1-1/2 hours or more, adding more juice and water, if necessary, during the cooking process. When the meat is tender, remove it from the pan along with the garlic cloves. Add to the sauce more orange juice and water, if necessary, to make about 1 cup (250 ml) of liquid. Add the raisins and capers and bring to a boil for several minutes to reduce the sauce slightly. Just before serving, add the almonds. Serve the meat with the sauce and garnish with the orange slices.

LOMO DE CERDO ADOBADO
Pork Loin in Chili Paste

Serves 6 to 8
10 *chiles anchos,* toasted, seeded and deveined
1 small onion, chopped
4 garlic cloves
1 teaspoon (5 ml) crushed dried oregano
1 teaspoon (5 ml) salt
1/4 cup (50 ml) white vinegar
3 pounds (1.5 kg) pork loin, cut into chops
1 tablespoon (15 ml) corn or safflower oil

Soak the chilies in boiling water to cover for 30 minutes. Drain the chilies and purée in a blender with the onion, garlic, oregano, salt and vinegar. Place the chops in a casserole or Dutch oven. Spread the chili paste on both sides of each chop and allow to marinate for 30 minutes. Place the chops in a preheated 350°F (180°C) oven and sprinkle the oil over them. Cover and cook until very tender, about 45 minutes to 1 hour, checking the meat from time to time and adding water as necessary to keep the chops from sticking to the pan.

COCHINITA PIBIL
Barbecued Pork

A kitchen version of the barbecue pits of Yucatán. Serve with hot tortillas and an uncooked sauce such as Mole de Barbacoa or Salsa Borracha.

Serves 6
1 2-inch (5 cm) square *achiote* paste, or
   2 tablespoons (30 ml) *achiote* seeds
2 tablespoons (30 ml) white vinegar
1/4 teaspoon (1 ml) cumin seeds, ground
1 teaspoon (5 ml) dried oregano
5 garlic cloves
1-1/2 teaspoons (8 ml) salt
3-1/2 to 4 pounds (1.5 to 2 kg) pork loin
1 large banana leaf (optional)
2 onions, thinly sliced

If you are using *achiote* seeds, simmer them in a small amount of water for 10 minutes, then soak overnight and crush in a mortar. Add the vinegar to the *achiote* paste or ground seeds, and purée in a blender with the cumin, oregano, garlic and salt.

Score the outside of the meat with a sharp knife, spread with the puréed mixture and marinate for 2 hours or more. If you are using a banana leaf, warm it in an oven set on low heat until it is flexible, and cut it crosswise, if necessary, to make a wrapping that will cover the meat completely. Place the meat on the banana leaf and cover the surface of the meat with the onion slices, fold the banana leaf over the meat to cover it completely, and tie tightly with cotton string. If you do not have a banana leaf, place the meat on a square of aluminum foil large enough to wrap the meat completely, cover the surface of the meat with the onion slices, and fold the foil over the meat, folding the edges over to make a tight package. Set the wrapped meat on a rack or a trivet in a Dutch oven, add cold water to a depth of 1 to 2 inches (3 to 5 cm), and bake in a preheated 350°F (180°C) oven for 4 to 5 hours, until the meat is so tender that it is falling from the bone (check the Dutch oven periodically, adding water as necessary to maintain the water level). Bring the meat to the table still in its wrapping, to be shredded and folded in hot tortillas.

POZOLE
Pork Stew with Hominy

A hearty country stew from Jalisco, often eaten, like *menudo*, after a night of too much revelry. This is an extravagant *pozole*; generally only a pig's head is used. If you cannot find pig's head in a market (check ethnic markets), ask your butcher to try to get it for you; if he cannot, substitute 1 pound (500 g) pork spareribs. Pigs' feet are available in many markets. *Nixtamal* hominy is made from the treated corn kernels that are ground into *masa* and should be available wherever *masa* is found; it is much superior to canned hominy and worth searching out.

Serves 10
6 *chiles anchos*, toasted, seeded and deveined
3 pigs' feet
1 pound (500 g) fresh *nixtamal* hominy or
   1 pound (500 g) canned hominy, drained
1 pound (500 g) pig's head, cut into pieces
1 pound (500 g) pork loin, cut into chops
1 2-1/2- to 3-pound (1.25 to 1.5 kg) chicken,
   cut into serving pieces
2 garlic cloves
2 teaspoons (10 ml) salt
1 large white onion, chopped
1 bunch radishes, sliced
Crushed dried oregano to taste (optional)
Chopped romaine lettuce
6 ounces (175 g) *queso fresco* or natural cream
   cheese, crumbled
Tostaditas

Place the chilies in hot water to cover and soak them overnight. The next day, remove any hair from the pigs' feet and scrub the feet well, then rinse. Place the feet in a saucepan with salted water to cover, bring to a boil, then reduce to a simmer. Cover and cook over low heat for several hours (3 or 4) until tender. Allow the feet to cool in the broth, then cut into serving sections; set aside.

Place the hominy in a large pot or saucepan. Add the meat and chicken and the cooked pigs' feet. Add cold water to cover and salt lightly. Bring the water to a boil, then reduce to a simmer and cover. Drain the soaked chilies, reserving the soaking water, and place them in a blender with the garlic and salt and blend to a smooth purée, adding a small amount of the soaking water if necessary. Add this purée to the hominy and meat and continue to cook until very tender, about 3 or 4 hours. Serve the *pozole* in deep plates and accompany with small dishes of onion, radishes, oregano, lettuce, cheese and *tostaditas*.

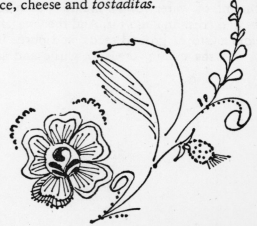

PIERNA DE CARNERO ENCHILADA
Roast Leg of Lamb with Chilies

Serves 8
4 *chiles anchos,* toasted, seeded and deveined
1 leg of lamb, about 5 pounds (2.5 kg)
4 ounces (100 g) pork fat (preferably fatback) or
  salt pork
3 garlic cloves
1 teaspoon (5 ml) salt
1/4 teaspoon (2 ml) freshly ground black pepper
1 tablespoon (15 ml) minced onion
2 tablespoons (30 ml) corn or safflower oil
Salt and freshly ground black pepper

Soak the chilies overnight in hot water to cover. The next day, trim excess fat from the leg of lamb and allow it to come to room temperature. Cut the pork fat or salt pork into thin strips. Mince 2 of the garlic cloves and mix with the salt and pepper. Roll the strips of pork fat in this mixture (if using salt pork, omit the salt). Lard the lamb with the fat or salt pork with a larding needle or by forcing the fat or salt pork into incisions made with a sharp knife. Drain the chilies, reserving the soaking water, and purée them in a blender with the remaining garlic clove, adding a small amount of the reserved water, if necessary, to make a thick paste. Spread the paste over the lamb, then sprinkle with the onion, oil and salt and pepper. Place in a preheated 350°F (180°C) oven and cook 25 minutes per pound for well-done lamb, 20 minutes per pound for slightly rare.

TERNERA EN NOGADA
Veal in Walnut Sauce

Serves 4 to 6
3 pounds (1.5 kg) veal shoulder or veal breast
2 medium onions
6 cups (1.5 L) water
4 garlic cloves
1 sprig thyme
1 teaspoon (5 ml) salt
2 tablespoons (30 ml) butter
1-1/4 cups (325 ml) walnuts, ground
1-1/2 cups (375 ml) heavy cream
Salt and ground white pepper to taste
1/4 cup (75 ml) toasted chopped almonds

Place the veal in a large saucepan with 1 of the onions, cut in quarters, and add the water, garlic, thyme and salt. Bring to a boil, skim, then reduce heat and cover and simmer until tender, about 1 hour. Allow the meat to cool in its broth, then remove from the pan, strain the broth and reserve. Cut the meat into thin strips and set aside. Mince the second onion and set aside. In a heavy skillet, heat the butter and cook and stir the minced onion until it is golden. Add the walnuts, cream, reserved veal broth and salt and pepper to taste. Bring to a simmer, add the veal, and maintain at a simmer until the sauce is slightly thickened. Serve sprinkled with the almonds.

PASTEL DE CONEJO
Rabbit Pie from San Luis Potosí

Serves 4 to 6

Filling
2 tablespoons (30 ml) butter
2 tablespoons (30 ml) corn or safflower oil
1 rabbit, cut into serving pieces
1 medium onion, sliced
1 sprig thyme
1 sprig marjoram
4 ounces (125 g) bacon, chopped
2 large leeks, chopped
1/2 onion, chopped
1-1/2 pounds (750 g) tomatoes, peeled, seeded
   and puréed
1/2 cup (125 ml) reserved rabbit broth
1/2 teaspoon (3 ml) crushed dried oregano
1/4 cup (50 ml) chopped pitted green olives
1/4 cup (50 ml) capers
Salt to taste

Pastry
4 eggs, separated
3 cups (700 ml) all-purpose flour
1 teaspoon (5 ml) baking powder
1/2 teaspoon (3 ml) salt
1/4 pound plus 3 tablespoons (150 g) butter, or
   1 cup (250 ml) heavy cream

1 egg yolk, mixed with
1 tablespoon (15 ml) water

To make the filling, heat the butter and oil together in a Dutch oven and brown the rabbit lightly on all sides. Add the onion and cook until tender. Add water to cover the rabbit, along with the thyme and marjoram. Bring to a boil, reduce the heat and cover and simmer until the rabbit is tender, about 1 hour. Allow the rabbit to cool in its broth. Remove the rabbit from the pan, reserving the broth, then remove the meat from the bones and chop coarsely; set aside. In a large, heavy skillet, cook the bacon until its fat is rendered, then add the leeks and onion and cook and stir until the onion is translucent. Add the puréed tomatoes and cook 3 to 4 minutes over medium heat, or until slightly thickened. Add the reserved rabbit broth, the chopped rabbit, oregano, olives and capers and simmer about 10 minutes until the flavors are blended and the mixture is thickened. Season to taste with salt.

To make the pastry, beat the egg whites until stiff; set aside. Sift the dry ingredients together; set aside. Cream the butter, then add the egg yolks one by one, mixing well. (If you are using cream in place of butter, beat the egg yolks together, then add the cream.) Stir the butter and egg mixture (or the cream and egg mixture) into the dry ingredients; immediately add the beaten egg whites and form the dough into a smooth ball. Divide the dough into 2 parts and roll each out on a floured board.

Place one pastry circle inside a buttered earthenware dish, fill with the filling and cover with the second pastry circle. Seal the edges, make 2 or 3 slashes in the pastry topping, and brush with the egg and water mixture to glaze. Bake in a preheated 350°F (180°C) oven until the crust is a golden brown, about 30 minutes. Cool slightly before serving, or serve at room temperature.

VENADO EN PIPIÁN
Venison Fricasee

In Campeche, this dish would be made with very small unhulled pumpkin seeds ground into the sauce, giving it a crunchier texture.

Serves 4 to 6

1 1-1/2-inch (4 cm) square *achiote* paste, or
   1 tablespoon (15 ml) *achiote* seeds
2 pounds (1 kg) young venison
4 garlic cloves
15 *epazote* leaves
1 cup (250 ml) unsalted hulled pumpkin seeds
6 *chiles anchos* or *mulatos*, toasted, seeded and
   deveined
2 cups (500 ml) water
1 pound (500 g) tomatoes, peeled, seeded and
   chopped
12 green plums, pitted and sliced (optional)
3 tablespoons (45 ml) *masa harina*
Salt to taste

If you are using *achiote* seeds, simmer them in a small amount of water for 10 minutes, then soak overnight. Grind in a mortar and set aside.

Remove as much fat as possible from the venison. Cut the meat into 2-inch (5 cm) cubes. Place in a large saucepan with water to cover and add 2 of the garlic cloves, crushed, and 5 of the *epazote* leaves. Bring to a boil, then reduce to a simmer, cover and cook until tender, 1-1/2 hours or longer, depending on the age of the animal.

When the meat is tender, place the pumpkin seeds in an ungreased heated pan and cook and stir until lightly toasted; watch carefully to prevent the seeds from burning. Allow the seeds to cool, then place in a blender with the chilies, the 2 remaining garlic cloves and the *achiote* paste or ground seeds. Grind all together, then add water. Slowly pour this mixture into the saucepan with the venison. With a large spoon, remove as much grease from the surface of the fricasee as possible, then add the tomatoes, the remaining *epazote* leaves and the plums. Mix the *masa harina* with a small amount of water and stir into the fricasee, then season to taste with salt. Allow the fricasee to simmer until the sauce is slightly thickened.

VEGETABLES

VEGETABLES *(Legumbres)*

The number of vegetables native to Latin America is amazingly large, including avocados, chilies, corn, chayotes, jícamas, potatoes, squash, tomatoes and wild greens among many others. These vegetables have become an integral part of the Mexican cuisine, and many vegetable dishes can be used as main courses, such as Aguacate Relleno de Picadillo and Aguacate Relleno de Queso, Calabacitas con Elotes, Chiles Rellenos and Chiles Rellenos con Queso, and Chiles en Nogada.

ESCABECHE DE CHILES MORRONES
Red Bell Peppers with Vinegar

This dish can be served warm as a vegetable or chilled and served with shredded romaine or leaf lettuce as a garnish for tacos, enchiladas, *quesadillas* and other dishes.

Serves 4 to 6
6 red or 3 red and 3 green bell peppers, roasted, peeled, seeded and deveined
1/2 cup (125 ml) olive oil
3 garlic cloves, crushed
1 large white onion, sliced
1/4 cup (75 ml) white vinegar or red wine vinegar
1/2 teaspoon (3 ml) crushed dried oregano
Salt and freshly ground black pepper to taste

Cut the peppers into thin strips or larger wedge-shaped pieces, as you like. In a heavy skillet, heat the oil and add the garlic cloves, cooking and stirring until golden; remove from the pan and discard. Add the sliced onion and peppers, and cook and stir until the onion is translucent. Remove from the heat, cool slightly, and add the vinegar, oregano and salt and pepper. Serve warm or cover and chill in the refrigerator.

CHILE RAJAS A LA CREMA
Chili Strips with Cream

Serves 4
3 *chiles poblanos*, roasted, peeled, seeded and deveined
1/4 cup (75 ml) corn or safflower oil
1 medium onion, minced
3 medium potatoes, cooked, peeled and cut into cubes
1 cup (250 ml) heavy cream
Salt and freshly ground black pepper to taste

Cut the chilies into thin strips and set aside. In a heavy skillet, heat the oil and cook and stir the onion until golden, then add the chili strips. When the oil turns a pale green, add the potatoes and cook and gently stir the potatoes a few minutes longer. Just before serving, add the cream and salt and pepper. Bring almost to a boil, stir gently and serve very hot.

CHILES CON CREMA Y ELOTE (Chilies with Cream and Corn) Follow the preceding recipe, substituting kernels cut from 3 ears of corn for the potatoes, and cooking the kernels with the chili strips for 10 minutes. After adding the cream, salt and pepper, stir in 1/2 cup (125 ml) shredded Monterey Jack cheese or 2 ounces (50 g) thinly sliced natural cream cheese.

CHILES RELLENOS
Chilies with Meat Filling

Serves 6

Filling
1 pound (500 g) pork shoulder or butt
1 pound (500 g) veal shoulder or breast
2 tablespoons (30 ml) lard or corn or safflower oil
1 medium onion, minced
12 ounces (325 g) tomatoes, roasted
1/4 cup (75 ml) slivered blanched almonds
1/4 cup (75 ml) pine nuts
3 tablespoons (45 ml) chopped *acitrón* or
   candied pineapple
2 tablespoons (30 ml) white vinegar
1/4 teaspoon (2 ml) ground cinnamon
Salt and freshly ground black pepper to taste
A pinch of sugar

Sauce
1-1/2 pounds (675 g) tomatoes, roasted
1 medium onion, minced
2 tablespoons (30 ml) reserved fat from the
   meat broth
2 cups (500 ml) reserved meat broth
1 cinnamon stick
Salt and freshly ground black pepper to taste

12 *chiles poblanos,* roasted and peeled
4 eggs, separated
1 cup (250 ml) lard or corn or safflower oil
1/4 cup (75 ml) flour
2 tablespoons (30 ml) minced parsley

To make the filling, cut the pork and veal into
2-inch (5 cm) squares and place in a large saucepan.
Add salted water to cover, bring to a boil, then
reduce to a simmer and cover partially. Cook until
the meat is tender, about 45 minutes. Allow the
meat to cool in the broth, then remove the meat
and set aside. Strain the broth and allow it to sit a

few minutes, then with a large spoon remove as much of the fat from the broth as possible; reserve both the broth and the collected fat. Shred the meat finely with a fork. In a large skillet, heat the 2 tablespoons (30 ml) lard or oil to the smoking point, add the meat and onion and cook and stir until the meat is lightly browned. Add the tomatoes and cook and stir over medium heat until the mixture is thickened, about 5 minutes. Add the remaining ingredients and cook 2 to 3 minutes longer, then taste and adjust the seasoning. Set aside and keep warm.

To make the sauce, purée the tomatoes and onion in a blender and then strain through a sieve, or purée in a food mill. In a medium saucepan, heat the 2 tablespoons (30 ml) reserved fat, add the tomato-onion purée and cook and stir over medium heat for 2 to 3 minutes. Add the reserved broth, bring to a boil and reduce to a simmer. Add the cinnamon stick, season to taste with salt and pepper and simmer, uncovered, for about 15 minutes.

Cut each chili open on one side, taking care not to cut through the top, or stem, section, and carefully remove the seeds and veins. Fill the chilies with the meat filling. Beat the egg whites until stiff, then beat the yolks lightly and fold them gradually into the beaten whites. In a large skillet, heat the lard or oil to the smoking point, dust each chili evenly with flour and then coat it evenly with the beaten eggs and fry until golden brown on all sides, turning carefully. Drain on absorbent paper. Remove the cinnamon stick from the tomato sauce, pour the sauce into a deep serving dish and add the hot, drained chilies; sprinkle with parsley and serve immediately.

CHILES RELLENOS CON QUESO (Chiles Stuffed with Cheese) Make the sauce for Chiles Rellenos, using lard or oil to fry the tomato-onion mixture. A light beef broth can be substituted for the pork broth. In place of the meat filling, stuff the chilies with thin slices of Monterey Jack cheese and proceed with the recipe as above.

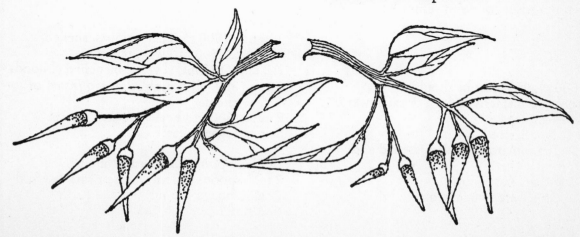

CHILES EN NOGADA
Chilies in Walnut Sauce

This famous dish from Puebla is a contrast in colors (green, red and white to represent the Mexican flag), flavors, textures and temperatures—the chilies are served very hot, covered with a cold sauce. Serve as a main course in summer.

Serves 6

Filling
1 pound (500 g) pork butt or shoulder
2 tablespoons (30 ml) lard or corn or safflower oil
2 garlic cloves, minced
1 medium onion, minced
1 pound (500 g) tomatoes, peeled, seeded and
  puréed
1/4 cup (75 ml) golden raisins
1/4 cup (75 ml) slivered blanched almonds

2 tablespoons (30 ml) minced *acitrón* or candied
  pineapple
1/4 teaspoon (2 ml) ground cinnamon
Salt and freshly ground black pepper to taste
2 small pears, peeled and cut in small dice
2 small peaches, peeled and cut in small dice
Sugar to taste (optional)

Sauce
1 pound (500 g) fresh walnuts, shelled, or
  2 cups (500 ml) walnut meats
1/2 cup (125 ml) slivered blanched almonds
1 cup (250 ml) crumbled *queso fresco* or
  feta cheese
2 cups (500 ml) heavy cream
Salt or sugar to taste

12 *chiles poblanos*, roasted and peeled
2 tablespoons (30 ml) corn or safflower oil
2 tablespoons (30 ml) minced parsley
Seeds of 1 pomegranate

To make the filling, cut the pork into 1-inch (3 cm) cubes. Place in a saucepan and add salted water to cover. Bring to a boil, reduce to a simmer, partially cover and cook until tender, about 45 minutes. Drain the meat, reserving the broth for another purpose. In a large skillet, heat the lard or oil, add the garlic and onion, and cook and stir until the onion is translucent. Add the meat and cook and stir until the meat is lightly browned. Stir in the tomato purée, raisins, almonds, *acitrón* or candied pineapple and cinnamon. Add salt and pepper to taste and simmer until thickened. Stir in the diced pears and peaches and simmer a few minutes longer. Add sugar to taste if you like. Set the filling aside and keep warm.

To make the sauce, cover the walnuts with warm water and let sit until the skins of the walnuts slip off easily. Remove all the skins by rubbing the walnuts between your fingers, then rinse and drain the walnuts. Place in a blender container with the almonds and cheese. Blend to a purée with a small amount of the cream, then add the remainder of the cream to make a smooth sauce. Season to taste with either salt or sugar, as you like. Place the sauce in the refrigerator and chill for at least 30 minutes.

To prepare the chilies, cut each one open on the side, keeping the top, or stem, portion of the chili intact, and carefully remove the seeds and veins. Dry the chilies on absorbent paper and stuff with the filling. In a large skillet, heat the oil over low heat and add the chilies. Cover the pan and heat the chilies for 2 or 3 minutes, then turn them, cover the pan and heat 2 to 3 minutes on the other side—the chilies should be heated through but should not brown. Drain briefly on absorbent paper, patting them with more absorbent paper to absorb the excess oil, and place in a warm shallow serving dish. Pour the cold walnut sauce over, sprinkle with the parsley and garnish the edges of the dish with pomegranate seeds; serve immediately.

QUELITES
Mustard Greens

Serves 4
2 *chiles poblanos,* roasted, peeled, seeded and
   deveined
1 pound (500 g) mustard greens
3 tablespoons (45 ml) lard or corn or safflower oil
2 tablespoons (30 ml) chopped onion
2 garlic cloves, chopped
8 ounces (250 g) tomatoes, peeled, seeded and
   chopped
Salt and freshly ground black pepper to taste
2 slices good white bread, crusts removed (optional)
Melted lard or corn or safflower oil to 1/4 inch
   (6 mm) (optional)

Cut the chilies into thin strips and set aside. Remove any tough stems from the mustard greens, then wash the greens well and cook in a very small amount of boiling water until just tender. In a heavy skillet, heat the lard or oil and cook and stir the onion and garlic until the onion is translucent. Add the chili strips and the tomatoes and cook over medium heat for 3 to 4 minutes. Add the mustard greens and salt and pepper and cook over low heat for 2 or 3 minutes to blend the flavors. Serve as is or prepare triangles of fried bread to serve with the greens: Cut the slices of bread into triangles. In a heavy skillet, heat the lard or oil to the smoking point and fry the bread quickly on both sides until golden; drain briefly on absorbent paper. Serve the greens adorned with the fried bread.

BUDÍN DE ELOTE
Corn Pudding

In place of the whipped cream, this soufflélike dish can be served with Chile Frito or Chile Rajas a la Crema without the potatoes.

Serves 4 to 6
6 ears of corn
1 cup (250 ml) milk
1/4 pound (125 g) butter, at room temperature
5 eggs, separated
1 teaspoon (5 ml) salt
A pinch of sugar
1/2 cup (250 ml) shredded Monterey Jack cheese
   (optional)
1/4 cup (75 ml) dry bread crumbs
3/4 cup (175 ml) heavy cream, whipped, seasoned
   with
Salt and ground white pepper to taste

With a sharp knife, cut the kernels off the ears of corn, then scrape the ears to collect the milky juice. Place the kernels and juice in a blender container and purée, adding as much of the milk as necessary to make a smooth purée; reserve any remaining milk. Cream the butter, then add the egg yolks one at a time, mixing well after each addition. Stir in the salt, sugar, optional cheese, corn and the reserved milk. Beat the egg whites until stiff, then fold them into the corn mixture. Heavily butter a 2-quart (2 L) ovenproof dish and sprinkle evenly with the bread crumbs. Pour in the pudding and bake in a preheated 350°F (180°C) oven until firm, about 45 minutes. Serve immediately, accompanied with the whipped cream.

CHAYOTES RELLENOS
Stuffed Chayotes

Chayotes are bumpy, pear-shaped vegetables belonging to the gourd family. They range in color from white to dark green; in the United States they are usually pale green.

Serves 6
3 chayotes, halved and seeded
2 tablespoons (30 ml) butter
1 small onion, minced
Salt and freshly ground black pepper to taste
1/2 cup (125 ml) fresh bread crumbs

Cook the chayotes in boiling salted water until tender, about 45 minutes. Scoop out the pulp, being careful not to tear the shells, and set the shells aside. Mash the pulp with a fork and set aside. In a heavy skillet, melt the butter and cook and stir the onion until translucent. Add the chayote pulp, onion and salt and pepper and cook and stir over low heat for 2 or 3 minutes. Stuff the chayote shells with this mixture, topping each half with a heaping tablespoonful (20 ml) of bread crumbs. Cook in a preheated 350°F (180° C) oven until the crumbs are golden; serve at once. Discard the inedible shells after eating the stuffing.

Tomatillos and chayotes

AGUACATE RELLENO DE PICADILLO
Avocados with Meat Filling

Avocados with a spicy meat filling, dipped in egg and fried, then served in a light tomato sauce.

Serves 6

Filling
1 pound (500 g) pork butt or shoulder, cut in chunks
1 tablespoon (15 ml) lard or corn or safflower oil
2 tablespoons (30 ml) minced onion
8 ounces (250 g) tomatoes, peeled, seeded and puréed
A pinch of ground cinnamon
A pinch of ground cloves
1/4 teaspoon (1 ml) ground cumin
Salt and freshly ground black pepper to taste
1 tablespoon (15 ml) capers
1 tablespoon (15 ml) minced parsley

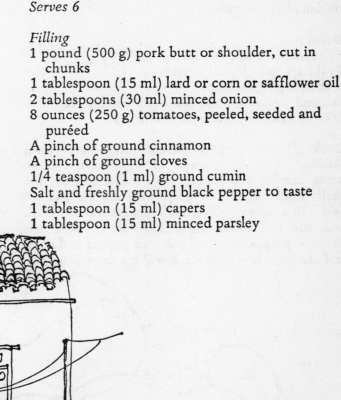

Pink church of Taxco

Sauce
1 tablespoon (15 ml) olive oil
1 pound (500 g) tomatoes, peeled, seeded and
  puréed
1 cup (250 ml) reserved pork broth
Salt to taste

3 large avocados, peeled and halved
3 eggs, beaten
A pinch of salt
Melted lard or corn or safflower oil to 1/2-inch
  (1 cm)

To make the filling, place the pork in salted water to cover, bring to a boil, reduce to a simmer and cook, partially covered, until tender, about 45 minutes. Let the meat cool in its broth, then remove, drain, and shred with a fork, reserving the broth. In a heavy skillet, heat the lard or oil to the smoking point, add the shredded pork and onion and cook and stir until the meat is lightly browned. Add the tomatoes, spices and salt and pepper and cook and stir over medium heat 3 to 4 minutes or until the mixture is thickened. Stir in the capers and parsley; set aside.

To make the sauce, heat the olive oil in a heavy skillet and add the tomato purée, cooking and stirring over medium heat for about 5 minutes. Add the reserved pork broth and simmer, uncovered, for 5 to 10 minutes, until slightly thickened. Season with salt to taste. Pour into a shallow serving dish and keep warm.

Spoon the filling into the avocado centers and press the filling down with the back of a spoon so that it is packed firmly and is level with the top of the avocado half. Mix the beaten eggs with the salt in a deep bowl. In a heavy skillet, bring the lard or oil almost to the smoking point. With a slotted spoon, dip each stuffed avocado half into the beaten eggs so that the avocado is completely coated with egg. Fry the avocados, filling side down, until lightly browned, then turn carefully with a spatula and brown the rounded sides of the avocados, turning with a wooden spoon to brown all over. Place the fried avocados in the warm tomato sauce and serve immediately.

AGUACATE RELLENO DE QUESO (Avocados Stuffed with Cheese) Follow the preceding recipe substituting 1 cup (250 ml) shredded Monterey Jack cheese for the meat filling.

BUDÍN DE CALABACITAS
Zucchini Pudding

Serves 4

1-1/2 pounds (750 g) small zucchini
2 *chiles poblanos,* roasted, peeled, seeded and
 deveined
1 tablespoon (15 ml) lard or corn or safflower oil
8 ounces (250 g) tomatoes, roasted and strained
Salt to taste
2 eggs, separated
1/4 cup (75 ml) heavy cream
4 ounces (125 g) Monterey Jack or natural
 cream cheese, thinly sliced
1 cup (250 ml) sour cream, mixed with
Salt to taste

Grate the zucchini, place in a colander, sprinkle with salt and allow to drain about 30 minutes, then squeeze the moisture from the zucchini by hand. Cut the chilies into thin strips and set aside. In a heavy skillet, heat the lard or oil and add the tomatoes along with the chili strips; cook and stir over medium heat 3 to 4 minutes. Season to taste with salt. Remove the mixture from the heat and cool to room temperature. Beat the egg whites until stiff; set aside. Beat the egg yolks until lemon-colored. Mix together the egg yolks, zucchini, cream and the cooled tomato-chili mixture. Fold in the beaten egg whites, taste and adjust seasoning, and pour into a heavily buttered 2-quart (2 L) ovenproof dish. Bake in a preheated 350°F (180°C) oven 30 minutes or until set. Arrange the slices of cheese evenly over the top of the pudding and return the pudding to the oven for a few minutes, until the cheese has slightly melted. Pour the salted sour cream over the pudding and serve at once, or pass the sour cream separately at table.

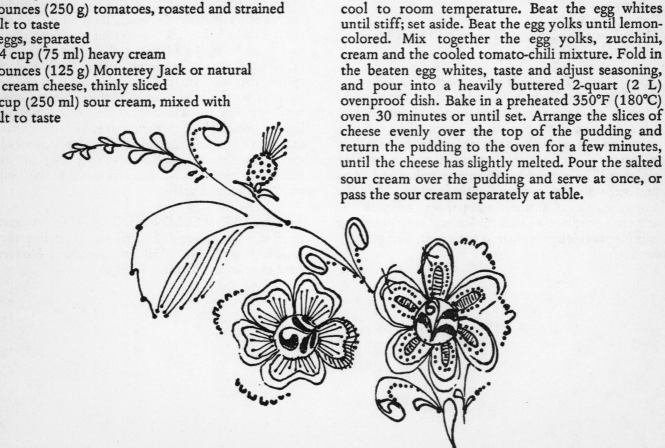

CALABACITAS CON ELOTES
Zucchini with Corn

This dish can serve as a main dish, along with beans or rice and a salad; to serve as a side dish, omit the pork and substitute 2 cups (500 ml) chicken broth for the pork broth.

Serves 4 to 6
2 pounds (1 kg) country-style pork spareribs
6 *chiles poblanos,* roasted, peeled, seeded and
   deveined
4 tablespoons (60 ml) lard or corn or safflower oil
12 ounces (325 g) tomatoes, roasted
1 onion, chopped
2 garlic cloves
6 ears of corn, cut into slices crosswise
1-1/2 pounds (750 g) small zucchini, cut in cubes
4 cups (1 L) reserved pork broth
Salt and freshly ground black pepper to taste
8 ounces (250 g) Monterey Jack or natural
   cream cheese, thinly sliced

Place the spareribs in a large saucepan with salted water to cover, bring to a boil, reduce heat to a simmer and cook, partially covered, until tender, about 45 minutes. Remove the spareribs from the pan with a slotted spoon and dry on absorbent paper. Measure the pork broth. If you have more than 4 cups (1 L), place the broth over high heat and boil until the amount of liquid is reduced to 4 cups (1 L). If you have less than 4 cups (1 L), add water to make that amount; set aside.

Cut the chilies into thin strips and set aside. In a large skillet, heat the lard or oil almost to the smoking point and fry the spareribs until lightly browned, adding the chili strips the last few minutes of cooking. Remove the skillet from the heat and with a large spoon collect and discard any excess oil; set the skillet aside. Purée the roasted tomato along with the onion and garlic in a blender or food mill. Add the corn, zucchini and the puréed tomato mixture to the spareribs and chilies and place over medium heat, stirring occasionally, until the sauce has thickened, about 5 minutes. Add the broth and season to taste with salt and pepper. Simmer the meat and vegetables, uncovered, 15 to 20 minutes or until the vegetables are tender and the sauce is thickened. Adjust the seasoning. Place the meat and vegetables in a large shallow serving dish and adorn with the slices of cheese; serve immediately.

BEANS & RICE

BEANS *(Frijoles)*

Almost as ubiquitous in Mexico as corn, beans combine with corn or rice to make a complete protein. Frijoles Estilo Mexicano can serve as a starch in place of rice or potatoes and, mashed and fried into Frijoles Refritos, can be used as an ingredient in countless tortilla dishes as well as serving as an appetizer. Chile con Carne, Frijoles Fronterizos and Frijoles a la Yucateca are all hearty enough for entrées. Note: Keep leftover beans refrigerated. If you have cooked them in an earthenware pot, transfer them to a metal saucepan to store in the refrigerator and reheat them in the saucepan the next day; a chilled earthenware pot will break if placed on heat.

FRIJOLES ESTILO MEXICANO
Mexican-Style Beans

Serves 6 to 8
1 pound (500 g) beans (red, pink, pinto or black)
6 cups (1.5 L) cold water
1 small onion, halved
1 tablespoon (15 ml) lard
2 teaspoons (10 ml) salt
2 tablespoons (30 ml) lard or corn or safflower oil
1 tablespoon (15 ml) chopped onion

Wash the beans and pick out any pebbles. Place them in a pot (preferably an earthenware pot) with the water and the onion. Bring the beans slowly to a boil, then cover and reduce to a simmer. When the beans begin to wrinkle, add the lard. When the beans have nearly cooked, add the salt without stirring, and continue cooking until they are very tender, about 1-1/2 to 2 hours in all.

Heat the 2 tablespoons (30 ml) lard or oil in another pot and cook the chopped onion until it is translucent. Add to the cooked beans and their liquid and simmer until the liquid has slightly thickened.

FRIJOLES REFRITOS
"Refried" Beans

To serve as an appetizer, insert *tostaditas* to cover the surface of the bean roll.

Serves 6
1/2 cup (125 ml) lard or corn or safflower oil
1/2 recipe Frijoles Estilo Mexicano (about 3 cups or 750 ml cooked beans)
Bean broth
Shredded Monterey Jack cheese, sliced natural cream cheese, *tostaditas,* fried and crumbled *chorizo* sausage, or thin slices of avocado

In a heavy skillet, heat the lard or oil over high heat. Add the beans in small amounts, along with a small amount of broth, mashing them quickly to a coarse paste with a bean masher or large spoon. Reduce heat to medium and cook until the beans begin to dry out and pull away from the skillet in a mass. Tilt the pan from side to side until the beans can be rolled out of the skillet like an omelet. Serve the beans very hot, on a heated plate, with any one or more of the suggested garnishes.

CHILE CON CARNE
Chilies and Beans with Meat

For a north-of-the-border version of this dish, add 1 pound (500 g) tomatoes, peeled, seeded and puréed, to the chili sauce, then cook the sauce with the meat as directed.

Serves 6 to 8
1 pound (500 g) pork butt or shoulder, cut in 1-inch (3 cm) cubes
4 *chiles anchos,* toasted, seeded and deveined
3 garlic cloves
1 onion, quartered
1/4 teaspoon (1 ml) cumin seeds
1/2 teaspoon (3 ml) crushed dried oregano
1/2 cup (125 ml) reserved chili water or more
2 tablespoons (30 ml) lard or corn or safflower oil
1 tablespoon (15 ml) flour
1 cup (250 ml) reserved pork broth
Salt to taste
1 recipe Frijoles Estilo Mexicano
Crumbled *queso fresco* or natural cream cheese (optional)
Chopped white onion (optional)

Place the meat in a large saucepan with salted water to cover, bring to a boil, reduce to a simmer and cook, partially covered, about 45 minutes or until tender. Drain the cooked meat in a colander or sieve, reserving the broth. While the meat is cooking, soak the chilies in hot water for 30 minutes. Drain the chilies, reserving the soaking water. Place the chilies in a blender container together with the garlic and onion. Grind the cumin seeds in a mortar, then add to the blender with the oregano and blend, adding the reserved soaking water as necessary to make a smooth sauce. In a large skillet, heat the lard or oil, add the flour and cook, stirring, just until the flour begins to brown lightly. Immediately add the chili mixture and cook and stir over medium heat for about 5 minutes. Add the cooked meat and reserved broth, season to taste with salt, cover the skillet and simmer 20 to 30 minutes until slightly thickened. Combine this mixture with the cooked beans in a large pot (the same one in which the beans were cooked, if it is large enough) and heat together several minutes to blend the flavors. Sprinkle crumbled cheese or chopped onions over individual servings, if you like.

FRIJOLES FRONTERIZOS
Frontier Beans

Beans with bacon, chilies, tomatoes and *chorizo* sausage. For a more *picante* flavor, substitute seeded, deveined and chopped *chiles serranos* for the *chiles poblanos*.

Serves 6 to 8
8 slices bacon
2 *chiles poblanos,* roasted, peeled, seeded, deveined and chopped
1 pound (500 g) tomatoes, peeled, seeded and chopped
1 recipe Frijoles Estilo Mexicano
2 *chorizo* sausages, thinly sliced
Queso fresco, Monterey Jack or natural cream cheese, thinly sliced
Sour gherkins or green or black olives

Brown the bacon in a heavy skillet; remove and drain on absorbent paper. In the bacon fat, cook the chopped chilies and the chopped tomatoes until tender. Add the beans with their broth and the sliced *chorizo.* Simmer, uncovered, until the broth has thickened slightly and the *chorizo* is cooked through. Serve the beans very hot, adorning with the slices of bacon and cheese, and the gherkins or olives.

Bean mashers

FRIJOLES A LA YUCATECA
Black Beans Yucatán Style

Save the bean broth from this dish to make Arroz Negro, if you like. To serve as a main course, increase the amount of pork to 1-1/2 to 2 pounds (750 g to 1 kg).

Serves 6 to 8
1 pound (500 g) black beans
2 teaspoons (10 ml) sea salt
8 ounces (250 g) pork butt, shoulder or
    country-style spareribs
1/2 teaspoon (3 ml) salt
4 tablespoons (60 ml) lard or corn or safflower oil
1 onion, minced
1 garlic clove, minced
2 cups (500 ml) reserved pork broth
Salt to taste
1/8 to 1/4 teaspoon (0.5 to 1 ml) *chile ancho* seeds
Minced white onion
Grated dry Monterey Jack or Parmesan cheese
Olive oil

Cook the beans as in the recipe for Frijoles Estilo Mexicano, using the sea salt in place of regular table salt. While the beans are cooking, cut the pork into chunks, place in a saucepan and barely cover with cold water; add 1/2 teaspoon (3 ml) salt. Bring to a boil, reduce heat, and simmer, uncovered, until the meat is tender, about 45 minutes. Allow the meat to cool in its broth, then drain the meat and measure the amount of broth. If necessary, add water to make 2 cups (500 ml) broth; if you have more, boil the liquid to reduce it slightly.

When the beans are tender, drain them (reserving the broth, if you like) and rinse them in cold water. Heat the lard or oil in a large pot or skillet and cook the onion and garlic until the onion is translucent. Add the beans and cook and stir for several minutes. Add the cooked pork and the 2 cups (250 ml) pork broth. Season to taste with salt. Grind the *chile ancho* seeds in a mortar or a spice grinder and season the beans to taste. Simmer the beans, uncovered, until slightly thickened. Serve adorned with the onion and cheese, and sprinkle a little olive oil over.

RICE (Arroz)

Rice was an important Spanish contribution to Mexican cookery, adding another source of protein to combine with corn and beans. Though rice is served as a separate course in Mexico, the following dishes have such a wide range of colors and flavors that they are perfect for serving with other foods. Arroz con Picadillo y Plátanos and Arroz con Pescado can be used as main courses.

ARROZ BLANCO
White Rice

Serves 6
2 cups (500 ml) long-grain rice
4 tablespoons (60 ml) lard or corn or safflower oil
1 medium onion, chopped
3 cloves garlic, minced
4 cups (1 L) hot water
1 sprig parsley
1 *chile poblano* or *serrano* (optional)
1 teaspoon (5 ml) salt

Soak the rice in hot water to cover for 15 minutes. Rinse in cold water until the water runs clear, then put to drain in a sieve. In a heavy skillet or flame-proof casserole with a lid, heat the lard or oil and cook the rice with the onion and the garlic, stirring constantly, until the rice is just opaque. Tip the pan and collect the excess lard or oil in a spoon; discard. Add the hot water, parsley, optional chili and salt, stirring once. Cover the rice and cook over low heat until spongy and almost dry, about 25 to 30 minutes.

ARROZ A LA MEXICANA
Rice Mexican Style

Serves 4
1-1/4 cups (325 ml) long-grain rice
4 tablespoons (60 ml) lard or corn or safflower oil
8 ounces (250 g) tomatoes, peeled, seeded and puréed
1 tablespoon (30 ml) minced onion
1 cup (250 ml) cold water
1/2 teaspoon (3 ml) salt
8 ounces (250 g) green peas, shelled
2 cups (500 ml) hot chicken broth
2 *chorizo* sausages
1 teaspoon (5 ml) minced parsley
2 avocados, peeled and thinly sliced

Soak the rice in hot water to cover for 15 minutes. Wash it in several changes of cold water until the water runs clear, then drain in a sieve. Heat the lard or oil and fry the rice, stirring constantly until the rice is opaque. Tip the pan and drain the excess lard or oil; remove with a spoon. Add the tomato purée and onion and cook over high heat, stirring, until the rice is almost dry. Add the cold water, salt and peas and simmer, uncovered, until the rice is again almost dry. Add the hot broth, cover the pot and simmer until the rice is dry and the grains are separate, about 25 or 30 minutes.

While the rice is cooking, remove the *chorizos* from their casings and fry in a heavy skillet until brown and crumbly. To serve, empty the cooked rice onto a platter and sprinkle the *chorizo* over, then the parsley, and garnish with slices of avocado.

ARROZ CON PICADILLO Y PLÁTANOS
Rice with Fried Meat and Plantains or Bananas

Serves 6
1 recipe Arroz Blanco
4 tablespoons (60 ml) lard or corn or safflower oil
1 tablespoon (15 ml) minced onion
1 pound (500 g) beef, finely chopped
8 ounces (250 g) tomatoes, peeled, seeded and
    puréed
1 tablespoon (15 ml) chopped parsley
1/4 cup (75 ml) golden raisins, plumped in water, or
    1/4 cup (75 ml) pitted green olives, chopped
1/4 cup (75 ml) slivered blanched almonds
Salt and freshly ground black pepper to taste
4 very ripe plantains or firm bananas
4 tablespoons (60 ml) corn or safflower oil

Prepare the Arroz Blanco and set aside. In a heavy skillet, heat the lard or oil and cook the onion and meat until the meat is well browned. Add the puréed tomato and the parsley and simmer for several minutes. Add the raisins or olives and the almonds and season to taste with salt and pepper.

Peel the plantains or bananas and halve lengthwise. In a heavy skillet, heat the oil and fry the plantains or bananas slowly until golden brown, turning them carefully. Serve the Arroz Blanco, meat and plantains or bananas on separate plates so that each guest can combine them to taste.

ARROZ VERDE
Green Rice

Serves 4 to 6
1-1/2 cups (375 ml) long-grain rice
4 tablespoons (60 ml) lard or corn or safflower oil
6 *chiles poblanos,* roasted, peeled, seeded and
    deveined
1 onion, chopped
1 garlic clove
4 cups (1 L) hot chicken broth
1/2 teaspoon (3 ml) salt
3 tablespoons (45 ml) butter
2 ounces (50 g) Monterey Jack or natural cream
    cheese, thinly sliced

Soak the rice in hot water to cover for 15 minutes. Rinse in cold water until the water runs clear, then put to drain in a sieve. In a heavy skillet, heat the lard or oil and cook and stir the rice until opaque. Tip the pan and collect the excess lard or oil in a spoon; discard. Purée the chilies with the onion and garlic in a blender or a food mill; add to the rice and cook over medium heat until the rice becomes almost dry. Add the hot broth and salt, cover the pot and cook over low heat until the rice is again almost dry, 10 or 15 minutes. Cut the butter into small strips and dot the top of the rice with them, then leave the rice on low heat until the rice is fully dry and the grains are separate, about 15 minutes. To serve, empty the rice onto a platter and adorn with the slices of cheese.

San Miguel

ARROZ AMARILLO
Yellow Rice

Serves 6
2 cups (500 ml) long-grain rice
4 tablespoons (60 ml) lard or corn or safflower oil
1 large onion, minced
3 garlic cloves, minced
8 ounces (250 g) tomatoes, peeled, seeded and
   puréed
4 cups (1 L) hot water or chicken broth
1/2 to 1 teaspoon (3 to 5 ml) salt
1 *chile serrano*, seeded, deveined and minced
   (optional)

Soak the rice in hot water to cover for 15 minutes. Rinse in cold water until the water runs clear, then put to drain in a sieve. In a heavy skillet or casserole with a lid, heat the lard or oil and cook the rice with the onion and garlic, stirring constantly, until the rice is golden. Tip the pan and collect the excess lard or oil in a spoon; discard. Add the tomato purée and continue to cook and stir for 2 or 3 minutes longer, then add the water or broth and the salt (add the larger amount of salt if you are using water rather than broth). Add the chili, if you like, bring to a boil, stirring once, then cover and simmer until almost dry, 25 to 30 minutes.

ARROZ NEGRO
Black Rice

Save the drained bean broth from Frijoles a la Yucateca to make this unique rice dish from Yucatán.

Serves 6
2 cups (500 ml) long-grain rice
4 tablespoons (60 ml) lard or corn or safflower oil
1 medium onion, minced
4 garlic cloves, minced
4 cups (1 L) hot broth from Frijoles a la Yucateca
Salt to taste
New green peas, artichoke hearts, shrimp, or
   chopped ham, pork or beef (optional)

Soak the rice in hot water to cover for 15 minutes. Rinse in cold water until the water runs clear, then put to drain in a sieve. In a heavy skillet or flameproof casserole with a lid, heat the lard or oil and cook the rice with the onion and garlic, stirring constantly until the rice is opaque. Tip the pan and collect the excess lard or oil in a spoon; discard. Add the hot bean broth and salt to taste. Add one or more of the optional ingredients, bring to a boil, stir once, then cover and simmer until almost dry, 25 to 30 minutes.

ARROZ CON PESCADO
Rice with Fish

Shrimp can be used in place of fish fillets in this dish.

Serves 6 to 8
2 cups (500 ml) long-grain rice
1/2 cup (125 ml) lard or corn or safflower oil
1-1/2 pounds (750 g) haddock fillets or
    any lean white fish fillets, cut in pieces
3 garlic cloves, crushed
2 pounds (1 kg) tomatoes, peeled, seeded and
    puréed
1 medium onion, minced
4 cups (1 L) hot water
1-1/2 teaspoons (8 ml) salt
4 sprigs cilantro, minced
2 sprigs mint, minced (optional)

Soak the rice in hot water to cover for 15 minutes. Rinse in cold water until the water runs clear, then put to drain in a sieve; set aside. In a heavy skillet, heat 4 tablespoons (60 ml) of the lard or oil almost to the smoking point and quickly fry the pieces of fish until lightly browned; drain on absorbent paper; set aside.

In another heavy skillet or a flameproof casserole with a lid, heat the remaining lard or oil and cook and stir the garlic cloves until just lightly browned, then remove and discard. Add the rice and cook and stir constantly until the rice is opaque. Tip the pan to drain the rice of excess oil; remove with a spoon. Add the tomatoes and onion and cook over medium heat until the rice is almost dry. Add the water, salt, cilantro and mint and bring the rice to a boil, stir once, then reduce to a simmer. Add the fish, distributing the pieces evenly through the rice. Cover and cook over low heat until the rice is almost dry, about 25 to 30 minutes.

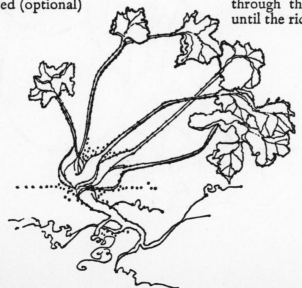

DESSERTS

DESSERTS *(Postres)*

More than any other category of food, Mexican desserts reflect the European influence on the cuisine. The Spanish brought sugar, wheat flour, chicken eggs, milk and cream and almonds to Mexico, and many of the more elaborate desserts popular today were perfected in convents by Spanish nuns. Some French and Austrian touches were added during the reign of Maximilian and Carlotta.

Remember that fresh fruits such as pineapples, mangos, papayas, bananas and oranges, sliced and sprinkled with sugar and lemon or lime juice or rum, are always good desserts for Mexican meals, alone or mixed with other fruits. Remember, also, Tamales de Dulce, to be served, like cookies, with a sweet drink in the afternoon or after a light meal.

PLÁTANOS FRITOS
Fried Plantains or Bananas

One of the simplest, and best, cooked fruit desserts. If you like, omit the sugar, rum and nutmeg and pour over Nuez de Miel.

Serves 4
4 very ripe plantains, or
    4 firm bananas
4 tablespoons (60 ml) butter
Grated *piloncillo* or dark brown sugar to taste
Dark rum to taste
Ground nutmeg (preferably freshly ground) to taste

Peel the plantains or bananas and cut them in half lengthwise. In a heavy skillet, heat the butter, add the plantains or bananas and cook over low heat until they are very tender, turning them carefully. Sprinkle with sugar, rum and nutmeg and serve hot.

ROLLOS DE COCO (Coconut Logs) Follow the preceding recipe, placing the plantains or bananas in a buttered ovenproof casserole. Pour over the juice of 1/2 lemon. Mix 1/2 cup (125 ml) grated coconut (preferably freshly grated) with grated *piloncillo* or dark brown sugar to taste and sprinkle over the fruit. Bake in a preheated 425°F (220°C) oven for 20 to 25 minutes, or until tender. Serve hot, with heavy cream to pour over, if you like.

CAMOTES MONICA
Sweet Potatoes Monica

Serves 4
2 pounds (1 kg) sweet potatoes or yams
1/2 cup (125 ml) honey
2 eggs, beaten
1/2 cup (125 ml) chopped peeled peanuts
A pinch of salt
Whole peeled peanuts

Cook the sweet potatoes or yams in salted boiling water to cover until they are tender, about 30 minutes; drain, cool, peel and purée in a food mill or force through a sieve. Mix the purée with the honey, then mix in the eggs, peanuts and salt. Mound this mixture in a buttered ovenproof casserole and place in a preheated 400°F (210°C) oven. Cook until a toothpick inserted in the center comes out clean. Serve warm, adorned with whole peeled peanuts.

DULCE DE PAPAYA
Papaya Sweet

Green papayas cooked to a thick, sweet paste. Good served hot or cold, with sweetened whipped cream.

Serves 8 to 10
9 small green papayas
2 pounds (1 kg) *piloncillo,* or
   4 cups (1 L) firmly packed dark brown sugar
Juice of 1/2 lemon

Halve and seed the papayas, then steam them, unpeeled, until just tender. Place the *piloncillo* or brown sugar in a very large, heavy saucepan, add the lemon juice and a small amount of water to dissolve the sugar, then cook over low heat until it begins to form a syrup. Scoop the papaya flesh from the shells and add to the syrup. Cook over low heat, stirring occasionally, until reduced to a very thick paste, 1-1/2 hours or longer.

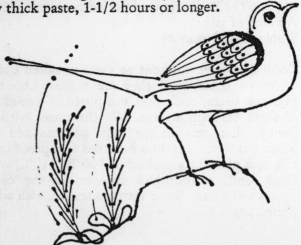

DURAZNOS CON ALMENDRA
Peaches with Almond Sauce

Serves 6
6 peaches
1-3/4 cups (425 ml) sugar
3 cups (750 ml) water
1 cinnamon stick
1/2 cup (125 ml) blanched almonds, ground
1 cup (250 ml) heavy cream
3 egg yolks, lightly beaten

Plunge the peaches into boiling water to cover for 15 seconds, then cool slightly in cold water and slip off the peels. Mix the sugar and the water in a saucepan and bring to a boil, stirring to dissolve the sugar. Add the cinnamon stick and the peaches and simmer, turning the peaches if necessary, until they are tender (pierce with a knife to test). Remove the peaches from the pan with a slotted spoon and place on a platter or individual serving dishes. Remove the cinnamon stick and boil the sugar syrup until it is reduced to about 1 cup (250 ml). Mix the ground almonds into the sugar syrup along with the heavy cream. Simmer this mixture for several minutes, then remove from heat. Mix 2 to 3 tablespoons (30 to 45 ml) of the hot liquid into the beaten egg yolks, then add the egg yolks to the syrup. Bring to a boil and cook for 2 to 3 minutes, stirring with a whisk. Allow the sauce to cool to room temperature, then pour over the peaches and serve.

CHONGOS ZAMORANOS
Sweet Curds and Whey, Zamora Style

An unusual dessert from Michoacan, similar to custard in texture. For a lighter curd, this dish can be made without the egg yolks.

Serves 6
3 egg yolks, beaten
6 cups (1.5 L) milk
2 rennet tablets
2 tablespoons (30 ml) water
1 cinnamon stick, lightly crushed
1 cup (250 ml) sugar

Mix the beaten egg yolks into the milk. Dissolve the rennet tablets in the water and add to the egg-milk mixture. Pour into an ovenproof baking dish and place over a pilot light or in a pan of hot water. When the milk has coagulated (about 30 minutes), cut the curd into six sections and sprinkle with the crushed cinnamon stick and the sugar. At this point the whey will begin to form. Place the baking dish in a pan of water over a very low flame and simmer the *chongos* for up to 2 hours, or until the whey and the sugar have formed a light syrup. Remove from heat and allow to cool to room temperature.

CAJETA ENVINADA
Sherry and Milk Dessert

Serves 6 to 8
1/2 cup (125 ml) blanched almonds
2 quarts (2 L) milk
2-1/3 cups (575 ml) sugar
3 egg yolks, lightly beaten
1 cup (250 ml) sherry
1/2 cup (125 ml) dark brown sugar (optional)

Grind the almonds in a nut grinder or a blender and mix with the milk and sugar in a saucepan. Bring to a boil over moderate heat, stirring to dissolve the sugar. Continue to boil, stirring occasionally, until thickened to the consistency of heavy cream, about 45 minutes. Remove from heat and allow to cool slightly. Stir 2 or 3 tablespoons (30 or 45 ml) of the mixture into the beaten egg yolks, then stir the egg yolks into the mixture in the saucepan. Return to the heat and simmer, stirring continually, until the *cajeta* has thickened so that it mounds in a spoon. Stir in the sherry and cook and stir a few more minutes; remove from heat and allow to cool slightly before pouring into a platter or individual serving dishes. If you like, sprinkle dark brown sugar over the *cajeta* and put under a broiler to glaze, watching carefully to keep the sugar from burning.

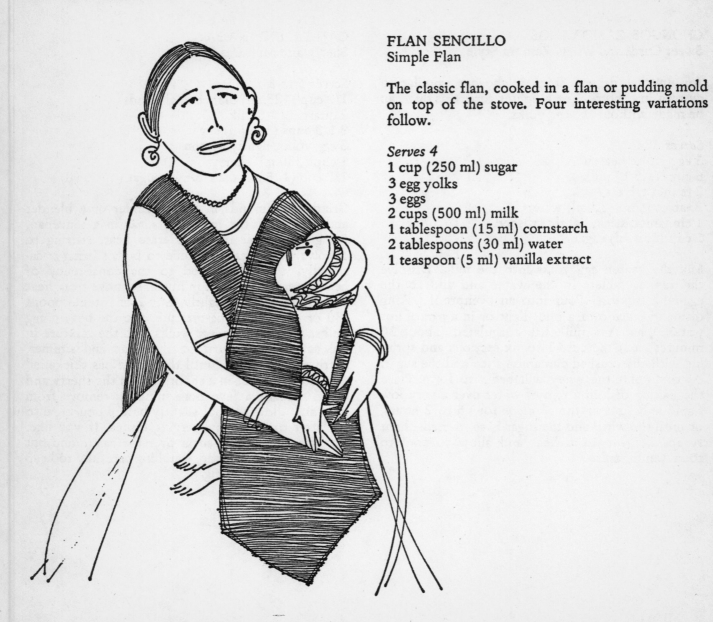

FLAN SENCILLO
Simple Flan

The classic flan, cooked in a flan or pudding mold on top of the stove. Four interesting variations follow.

Serves 4
1 cup (250 ml) sugar
3 egg yolks
3 eggs
2 cups (500 ml) milk
1 tablespoon (15 ml) cornstarch
2 tablespoons (30 ml) water
1 teaspoon (5 ml) vanilla extract

Place 1/2 cup (125 ml) of the sugar into a heavy pan over high heat (do not use unenameled cast iron or tinned copper). Stir the sugar constantly with a wooden spoon until it begins to foam and turn a deep golden brown; be careful not to let it burn. Immediately pour the caramel into a flan or pudding mold, turning it quickly so that the caramel coats the bottom and the sides of the mold; allow to cool. Beat the yolks and whole eggs together until they thicken slightly; set aside. Place the milk in a saucepan and bring to a boil over moderate heat. Mix the remaining 1/2 cup (125 ml) sugar into the milk, then dissolve the cornstarch in the water and add this mixture to the milk. Add the milk little by little to the beaten eggs, beating continually. Add the vanilla and mix well.

Pour the mixture into a flan or pudding mold. Grease the underside of a tightly fitting lid and cover the mold. (If you do not have a tightly fitting lid, cut a circle of aluminum foil slightly larger than the top of the mold, butter the underside and fit over the mold, topping with any lid that will barely fit into the mold so that the foil makes an airtight cover.) Place the mold in a pan with water about halfway up the sides of the mold. Cook at a low simmer, taking care that no water splashes up into the mold and that the water does not burn dry. Cook until the flan is set, 1-1/2 to 2 hours; a knife inserted into the center should come out clean. Remove the flan from the heat and cool to room temperature. If the flan is kept in the refrigerator, be sure it is at room temperature before you unmold and serve it.

FLAN DE NARANJA (Orange Flan) Follow the recipe for Flan Sencillo, using freshly squeezed and strained orange juice in place of the milk, and grated orange peel to taste in place of the vanilla extract.

FLAN DE PINA (Pineapple Flan) Follow the recipe for Flan Sencillo, using pineapple juice in place of the milk and boiling the pineapple juice with the 1/2 cup (125 ml) sugar for the flan. Allow the pineapple juice to cool slightly before adding the dissolved cornstarch and mixing with the eggs.

FLAN DE COCO (Coconut Flan) Grate one-half of the meat of a small coconut and place in a saucepan with 1/2 cup (125 ml) water and 1/2 cup (125 ml) of the sugar for the flan. Simmer until the grated coconut becomes translucent; set aside. Follow the recipe for Flan Sencillo, adding the grated coconut and its cooking liquid to the boiled milk along with the remaining sugar.

FLAN DE NUEZ (Nut Flan) Grind 1 cup (250 ml) walnuts, pine nuts, blanched almonds or toasted filberts in a nut grinder and set aside. (If using almonds, they can be ground in a blender.) Follow the recipe for Flan Sencillo, adding the ground nuts to the boiled milk along with the sugar.

CAJETA DE LECHE DE CELAYA
Milk Confection from Celaya

This is a thick, very sweet confection that is eaten with a spoon (it is also known as *dulce de leche*). The goat's milk gives it a musky flavor and taste; it can be made entirely with cow's milk, if you prefer. This recipe may be halved, but you may want to make the full amount, as *cajeta* will keep almost indefinitely if refrigerated in tightly sealed jars. Figure on 1/2 cup (125 ml) or less per serving. This *cajeta* is light in color; Leche Quemada, the variation following, is a rich, dark caramel color.

Makes about 6 cups (1.5 L)
6 cups (1.5 L) goat's milk
6 cups (1.5 L) cow's milk
1/2 teaspoon (3 ml) baking soda
1 teaspoon (5 ml) cornstarch
3 cups (750 ml) sugar

Place the goat's milk and 5 cups (1.25 L) of the cow's milk into a very large, heavy saucepan over moderate heat and bring to a boil. Mix the baking soda and cornstarch together and add the remaining cup of milk, very slowly at first, stirring to dissolve the dry ingredients; add this mixture to the boiling milk. Stir in the sugar with a wooden spoon until the sugar is dissolved. Boil the mixture until it is slightly thickened (to the consistency of heavy cream). Continue to boil the *cajeta,* stirring constantly, until it has thickened so that it forms a ribbon when poured from a spoon. Pour into a platter or individual bowls and cool before serving.

LECHE QUEMADA (Burned Milk) Place the sugar in a large, heavy saucepan and mix in 1 cup (250 ml) of the milk. Cook over medium heat, stirring constantly, until the sugar caramelizes to a light golden color. Remove from heat and set aside. Place the baking soda and cornstarch into a large saucepan and pour in, very slowly at first, 1 cup (250 ml) of the milk, stirring to dissolve the dry ingredients. Stir in the remaining 10 cups (2.5 L) milk and place over moderate heat, bringing the mixture to a boil. Pour the boiled milk into the caramelized sugar mixture, stirring well, and boil over moderate heat until it thickens to the consistency of heavy cream. Continue to boil, stirring constantly, until it has thickened so that it forms a ribbon when poured from a spoon. Pour into a platter or individual bowls and cool before serving.

ARROZ CON LECHE
Rice Pudding

A creamy rice pudding, cooked on top of the stove.

Serves 4 to 6
1/4 cup (75 ml) golden raisins
1 cup (250 ml) long-grain rice
2 cups (500 ml) water
A pinch of salt
2 strips lemon peel
2 cups (500 ml) milk
1 cinnamon stick, or
   1 1-inch (3 cm) piece vanilla bean
3/4 cup (175 ml) sugar
2 egg yolks, lightly beaten
Ground nutmeg (preferably freshly ground) or
   ground cinnamon to taste (optional)

Soak the raisins in a small amount of water to plump them; set aside. Soak the rice in hot water to cover for 15 minutes, then drain and wash well in cold water until the water runs clear. In a heavy saucepan, bring the 2 cups (500 ml) water to a boil and add the salt, lemon peel and rice. Reduce heat and simmer, covered, until almost dry, about 20 minutes. Heat the milk over low heat with the cinnamon stick or vanilla bean until almost scalded, stir into the rice with the sugar and simmer, uncovered, until most of the milk is absorbed. Remove the cinnamon stick or vanilla bean. Remove the rice from the heat, cool slightly, then stir in the egg yolks, return to heat and cook until slightly thickened, stirring occasionally to keep the pudding from sticking to the bottom of the pan. Drain the raisins and stir into the pudding; pour the pudding onto a serving platter, sprinkling with ground nutmeg or cinnamon to taste, if you like.

BUÑUELOS
Fritters in Syrup

These fritters can also be made without the aniseed and syrup; sprinkle them with ground cinnamon and sugar or pour over Nuez de Miel.

Makes 18

Syrup
1 pound (450 g) *piloncillo,* or
    2 cups (500 ml) dark brown sugar, packed
1 cup (250 ml) water
1 teaspoon (5 ml) aniseed

Fritters
1 cup (250 ml) water
1 teaspoon (5 ml) aniseed
3-1/2 cups (825 ml) all-purpose flour
1 teaspoon (5 ml) baking powder
1/2 teaspoon (2 ml) salt
2 eggs
1 cup (250 ml) corn or safflower oil

To make the syrup, dissolve the *piloncillo* or the brown sugar in a saucepan with the water. Add the aniseed and bring the mixture to a boil; continue boiling until the syrup thickens slightly. Remove from heat and pour through a strainer to remove the aniseed, then set aside to cool.

To make the fritters, bring the water to a boil with the aniseed. Remove from heat and set aside to cool; do not strain. Sift the flour with the baking powder and salt. Add the eggs and enough aniseed water to make a firm dough. Knead the dough well, until it is smooth. Divide into 18 pieces, form into balls, and roll out on a floured board into circles about 1/2-inch (1 cm) thick. Place the dough circles on a floured surface and allow them to dry slightly, about 30 minutes. In a heavy skillet, heat the oil to the smoking point and fry the fritters until puffed and golden, then remove from the fat and drain on absorbent paper. Serve them warm, with the reserved syrup poured over or passed separately.

BUDIN DE GARBANZO
Garbanzo Cake

A firm-textured cake from Queretaro, to serve with sliced fresh fruit such as oranges, pineapples or mangos. A thin icing made of lemon juice and powdered sugar can replace the sprinkling of sugar —allow the icing to drip partially down the sides of the cake.

Makes 8 servings
1 cup (250 ml) dry garbanzo beans
4 eggs, beaten
1 cup (250 ml) sugar
1/2 teaspoon (3 ml) baking powder
Grated rind of 1 large lemon
Sifted powdered sugar

Soak the garbanzo beans overnight in water to cover. The next day, place in a saucepan with salted water to cover. Bring to a boil, then cover and reduce to a simmer and cook until the beans are tender, from 1 to 2 hours. Wash them in a sieve under cold running water, rubbing the beans between your fingers to remove the skins. Purée the beans in a blender or a food mill. Add the eggs, sugar, baking powder and lemon rind to the bean purée, mixing well.

Butter a 9-inch (23 cm) cake pan or a pudding or charlotte mold. Cut a circle of heavy brown paper to fit the bottom of the cake pan or mold, butter the paper on both sides and fit it into the bottom of the pan or mold. Pour in the cake batter and place in a preheated 350°F (180°C) oven. Cook until a toothpick inserted into the center of the cake comes out dry, about 45 minutes for the cake pan and 1 hour or more for the mold. Cool on a rack for 15 minutes, then remove from pan or mold and cool to room temperature before serving. Serve with powdered sugar sprinkled over the top.

GALLETITAS DE NUEZ
Walnut Cookies

Nut cookies from Michoacan. Serve with fresh fruit or Rompope.

Makes about 5 dozen
1/2 pound (250 g) butter, at room temperature
3/4 cup (175 ml) sugar
1 cup (250 ml) walnuts
2 cups (500 ml) all-purpose flour
Sifted powdered sugar

Cream together the butter and sugar. Grind the walnuts in a nut grinder and add with the flour to the butter-sugar mixture, mixing well. Chill the dough for 1 hour. Form the dough into two rolls 1 inch (3 cm) in diameter and cut each cookie 1/4-inch (6 mm) thick. Place on greased cookie sheets in a preheated 350°F (180°C) oven for 15 minutes. Allow to cool slightly and dip in powdered sugar.

BEVERAGES

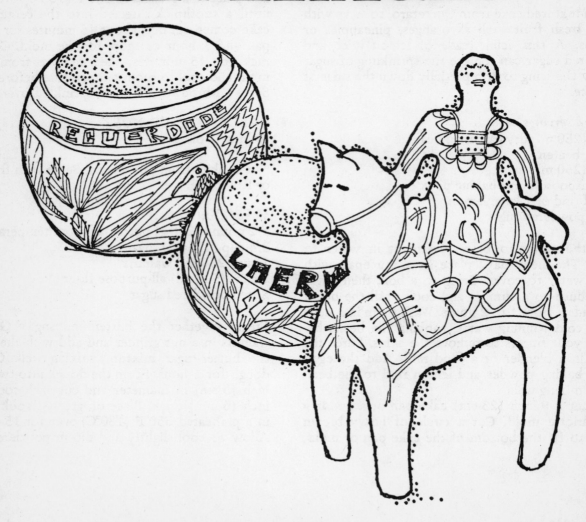

BEVERAGES *(Bebidas)*

Coffee and chocolate, in their distinctively Mexican versions, can be served with pastries at breakfast or in the afternoon, with egg dishes for brunch, and after dinner. Serve mixed drinks made with tequila with appetizers, Sangría or Mexican beer with dinner, and Rompope or a coffee liqueur as an after-dinner drink.

CAFÉ DE OLLA
Coffee in an Earthenware Pot

The traditional way of making coffee in Mexico. Try a Mexican coffee in this recipe—two of the best are Altura Coatepec and Oaxaca Pluma.

Makes 4 cups (1 L)
1 quart (1 L) water
Grated *piloncillo* or dark brown sugar to taste
3/4 cup (175 ml) finely ground dark-roasted coffee

Heat the water in a pot, preferably made of earthenware, and add the *piloncillo* or brown sugar. Stir to dissolve the sugar and add the coffee. Bring the coffee to a boil, allow to boil 1 minute and then remove from heat. Stir to mix the coffee well, then cover the pot, keeping it warm until the coffee grounds have settled to the bottom. Pour through a fine sieve or a filter and serve, preferably in earthenware mugs.

CAFÉ CON LECHE (Coffee with Milk) Mix hot milk in proportions of 3 parts milk to 1 part coffee.

CHAMPURRADO
Chocolate *Atole*

Atole is an ancient Indian corn drink traditionally served with tamales in Mexico. Like Chocolate en Leche and Café de Olla, it is thought to taste best when made in an earthenware pot.

Makes 8 cups (2 L)
6 cups (1.5 L) milk
3 ounces (75 g) Mexican chocolate
1 cup (250 ml) *masa harina*
2 cups (500 ml) water
1 cinnamon stick
Grated *piloncillo* or dark brown sugar to taste

In a large saucepan, heat the milk with the chocolate, stirring to dissolve the chocolate; set aside and keep warm. Mix the *masa harina* with the water and pour into a pot, preferably made of earthenware. Place the pot over low heat, add the cinnamon stick and cook until the *masa* becomes translucent. Add the milk and chocolate mixture and stir in sugar to taste. The *chapurrado* should be of a thin gruel-like consistency; you may thin it further with milk at this point, if you like. Heat a few minutes and serve hot, preferably in earthenware mugs.

CHOCOLATE EN LECHE
Chocolate in Milk

Mexican chocolate is a mixture of chocolate, sugar, cinnamon and ground almonds, and is sold packaged in tablets sectioned into triangles. It is traditionally heated in a deep earthenware pot, or *olla*, and whirled to a froth with a *molinillo*, a carved wooden implement that is twirled between the palms of the hands. Serve for breakfast and in the late afternoon with sweet pastries.

Makes 4 cups (1 L)
6 ounces (175 g) Mexican chocolate
4 cups (1 L) milk

Put the chocolate and milk into a pot, preferably made of earthenware, and heat to a boil, stirring occasionally to mix in the melting chocolate. Remove from the heat, then return and allow to come to a boil again. Beat with a *molinillo* or whisk until frothy, or put into a blender and blend a few seconds at high speed. Serve in earthenware mugs.

CHOCOLATE EN AGUA (Chocolate in Water) Place 2 cups (500 ml) water in a pot, preferably made of earthenware, and bring to a boil. Add the chocolate and stir to mix in the melting chocolate. When the chocolate is thoroughly melted, add 2 cups (500 ml) water and allow the mixture to come again to a boil. Beat or blend as above.

ROMPOPE
Eggnog Drink

Serve this rich drink in liqueur glasses after dinner or in the late afternoon, accompanied with sweet pastries or candies, if you like.

Makes about 2 quarts (2 L)
1-1/2 quarts (1.5 L) milk
2 cups (500 ml) sugar
1 cinnamon stick, or
   1 1-inch (3 cm) piece vanilla bean
15 egg yolks
1 pint (500 ml) amber rum

Molinillo

Put the milk, sugar and cinnamon stick or piece of vanilla bean in a pan and bring to a boil, stirring constantly. Regulate the heat so that the mixture continues to boil steadily and allow it to boil for about 10 minutes, or until it has reduced by about one-third; stir frequently during this time. Remove from the heat and cool to lukewarm. Beat the egg yolks lightly and mix into the milk-sugar mixture. Return to heat, bring again to a boil, and cook the mixture until slightly thickened. Remove from heat and allow to cool somewhat; stir in the rum. Beat with a *molinillo* or a whisk until frothy, or blend a few cups at a time in a blender. Allow to cool to room temperature, then pour into sterilized glass bottles. Cap and store in the refrigerator, where it will keep for several weeks.

SANGRÍA
Wine Punch

Makes 5 cups (1.25 L)
2 cups (500 ml) water
2 tablespoons (30 ml) sugar, or to taste
2 cups (250 ml) fresh orange juice
1 cup (250 ml) dry red wine
2 tablespoons (30 ml) fresh lemon juice
Coarsely crushed ice
Strips of lemon peel (optional)

Place the water in a glass pitcher and add the sugar, stirring to dissolve. Add the orange juice, wine and lemon juice. Serve poured over crushed ice, garnished with strips of lemon peel, if you like.

COCTEL DE TEQUILA
Tequila Cocktail

Serves 4
1 egg white
5 ounces (150 ml) fresh lemon juice
3 tablespoons (45 ml) grenadine
8 ounces (250 ml) white tequila
Coarsely crushed ice

Place the egg white, lemon juice and grenadine into a cocktail shaker and shake until well mixed. Add the tequila and crushed ice and shake until very cold. Alternately, place all the ingredients in a blender container and blend at high speed until frothy. Serve in a chilled glass pitcher.

SANGRITA
Tomato-Chili Drink

This *picante* concoction is served in a small glass, accompanied with a small glass containing 1 ounce (30 ml) of tequila, and the two liquids are drunk alternately.

Serves 1
1/2 cup (125 ml) chilled tomato juice
1 tablespoon (15 ml) fresh orange juice
1 wedge lemon or lime
2 teaspoons (10 ml) minced onion
Powdered *chile pequin* to taste
Salt to taste

Mix the tomato and orange juice, squeeze the wedge of lemon or lime into the drink and drop in the rind. Stir in the onion and add chili and salt to taste. Serve in a chilled glass.

COCTEL DE MARGARITA
Margarita Cocktail

Although its Mexican origins have been questioned, the margarita very probably evolved from the Mexican custom of drinking straight tequila with salt and a wedge of lime. You can use Cointreau or white Curaçao in place of Triple Sec in this recipe, as they are all virtually the same orange liqueur.

Serves 1
1 wedge of lime
1 saucer of sea salt
2 ounces (50 ml) white tequila
1 tablespoon (15 ml) Triple Sec
2 tablespoons (30 ml) fresh lime juice
1/2 teaspoon (3 ml) superfine sugar
Coarsely crushed ice

Rub the rim of a cocktail glass with the wedge of lime; reserve the lime. Dip the rim of the glass in the saucer of salt to evenly coat the rim with salt. Shake the tequila, Triple Sec, lime juice and sugar in a cocktail shaker, or for a frothier margarita, blend at high speed in a blender. Serve strained or over ice, adding the reserved wedge of lime.

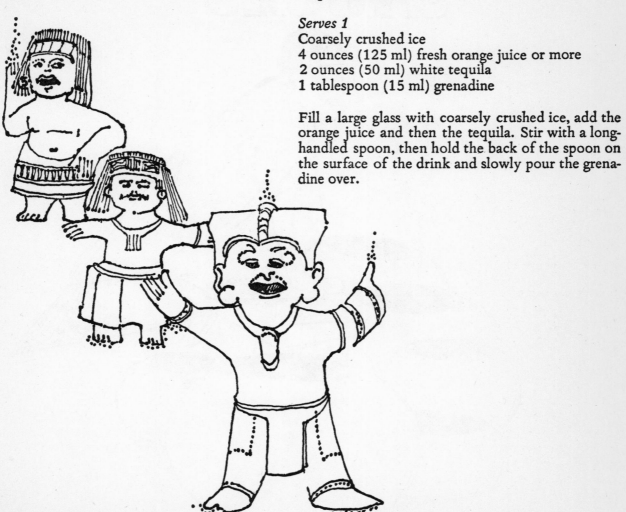

TEQUILA Y NARANJA
Tequila Sunrise

Serves 1
Coarsely crushed ice
4 ounces (125 ml) fresh orange juice or more
2 ounces (50 ml) white tequila
1 tablespoon (15 ml) grenadine

Fill a large glass with coarsely crushed ice, add the orange juice and then the tequila. Stir with a long-handled spoon, then hold the back of the spoon on the surface of the drink and slowly pour the grenadine over.

SAUCES

SAUCES *(Salsas)*

The following recipes include both cooked and uncooked sauces as well as two dessert sauces. The three guacamoles in the Appetizer section also make excellent sauces, as do the sauces for Tostaditas con Chile Ancho and Enchiladas de Queso.

SALSA DE JITOMATE
Uncooked Tomato Sauce

This is the basic Mexican table sauce, to be used with almost everything from *tostaditas* to main dishes. With the addition of the optional vinegar, it can serve as a sauce and as a dressing for chopped lettuce as well. It is best when made fresh, but can be kept in the refrigerator.

Makes about 3 cups (750 ml)
1 pound (500 g) tomatoes, seeded and minced
2 *chiles serranos,* seeded, deveined and minced
1 white onion, minced
1 tablespoon (15 ml) minced cilantro
2 tablespoons (30 ml) corn or safflower oil
2 tablespoons (30 ml) white vinegar (optional)
Salt and freshly ground black pepper to taste

Mix all the ingredients together. Serve at the table to be added to food to taste.

SALSA DE CHILE PASILLA
Pasilla Chili Sauce

A *picante* sauce to serve at the table. It is very good with Frijoles Estilo Mexicano or a bowl of bean broth.

Makes about 1 cup (250 ml)
1 tablespoon (15 ml) lard or corn or safflower oil
3 *chiles pasillas*
3 tablespoons (45 ml) olive oil
2 tablespoons (30 ml) white vinegar
1 teaspoon (5 ml) crushed dried oregano
Salt to taste
1/4 cup (75 ml) grated dry Monterey Jack or
    Parmesan cheese or to taste

Heat the lard or oil in a heavy skillet and cook the chilies until they change color, turning constantly and taking care not to burn them. Drain them on absorbent paper and allow them to cool, then remove the seeds and veins and purée the chilies in a blender with the oil, vinegar, oregano and salt. Serve in a bowl at the table with the cheese floated on top, if you like, or serve the cheese separately.

SALSA DE TOMATE VERDE
Husk Tomato Sauce

An uncooked *tomatillo* table sauce to be used, like Salsa de Jitomate, on almost everything. Use the cooked version as a *salsa verde* for enchiladas and other tortilla dishes.

Makes about 2 cups (500 ml)
1 pound (500 g) *tomatillos,* husked, or
   2 cups (500 ml) canned *tomatillos,* drained
3 *chiles serranos,* seeded, deveined and chopped
1 small onion, chopped
2 garlic cloves
1 tablespoon (15 ml) minced cilantro
A pinch of sugar
Salt to taste

If you are using fresh *tomatillos,* cook them in a small amount of boiling salted water until tender, about 10 minutes; drain. Purée the *tomatillos,* chilies, onion and garlic in a blender or food mill. Add the cilantro and sugar and season to taste with salt.

SALSA DE TOMATE VERDE COCIDA (Cooked Husk Tomato Sauce) If you are using fresh *tomatillos,* cook them as directed above, together with the chilies. If you are using canned *tomatillos,* cook the chilies alone in a small amount of boiling salted water until tender, then drain. For a milder sauce, substitute 1 large *chile poblano,* roasted, peeled, seeded and deveined, for the *serrano* chilies. Purée the *tomatillos* and chilies with the onion, garlic and cilantro. In a heavy skillet, heat 2 tablespoons (30 ml) lard or corn or safflower oil, add the purée and cook and stir 3 to 4 minutes, until slightly thickened, then add the sugar and salt.

SALSA DE CHIPOTLE Y AGUACATE
Chipotle Chili and Avocado Sauce

An uncooked sauce that is good with almost anything.

Makes about 4 cups (1 L)
1 pound (500 g) tomatoes, roasted and strained
3 *chiles chipotles* in vinegar, drained, seeded and deveined
3 medium avocados
1 tablespoon (15 ml) minced onion
1 tablespoon (15 ml) olive oil
Crushed dried oregano to taste
Salt to taste

Purée the tomatoes with the chilies in a blender. Peel and seed the avocados and cut into small dice. Mix with the tomato-chili purée. Add the onion, oil, oregano and salt to taste.

MOLE DE BARBACOA
Barbecue Sauce

This is a very simple fresh sauce for barbecuing. This amount is enough for 2 to 3 pounds (1 to 1.5 kg) meat or chicken.

Makes about 3 cups (750 ml)
2 pounds (1 kg) tomatoes, roasted and strained
1 garlic clove
1 small white onion, chopped
1 sprig cilantro
Minced *chiles serranos* to taste
Salt to taste

Purée the tomatoes with the garlic, onion and cilantro in a blender. Add water to the mixture to make a smooth, fairly thin sauce. Add chilies to taste.

SALSA BORRACHA
Drunken Sauce

A wonderful sauce for charcoal-cooked chicken and meat.

Makes about 2 cups (500 ml)
6 *chiles anchos* or *mulatos,* toasted, seeded and deveined
3/4 cup (175 ml) white tequila
3/4 cup (175 ml) fresh orange juice
1 tablespoon (15 ml) minced onion
1 tablespoon (15 ml) olive oil
1/2 teaspoon (2 ml) salt

Soak the chilies in warm water until soft. Drain and purée them in a blender, adding the tequila and orange juice to the purée to make a smooth sauce. Add the onion, oil and salt.

CHILE FRITO
Cooked Tomato-Chili Sauce

A basic tomato sauce from Campeche.

Makes about 4 cups (1 L)
2 pounds (1 kg) tomatoes, peeled and seeded
1 *chile serrano,* seeded and deveined
4 tablespoons (60 ml) lard or corn or safflower oil
1 small onion, minced
1 sprig *epazote* (optional)
1/2 cup (125 ml) water or more
Salt to taste

Purée the tomatoes and the chili in a blender or food mill. In a heavy skillet, heat the lard or oil. Add the tomato-chili purée, the onion and *epazote* and cook and stir 5 minutes or more, until thickened. Add water as necessary to make a smooth sauce, salt to taste, and simmer several minutes longer.

SALSA DE CHILE Y CEBOLLA
Tomato-Chili Sauce with Onion

A rich, *picante* cooked sauce.

Makes about 3 cups (750 ml)
3 *chiles anchos,* toasted, seeded and deveined
1 large white onion, sliced or chopped
1 pound (500 g) tomatoes, roasted and strained
3 tablespoons (45 ml) lard or corn or safflower oil
2 tablespoons (30 ml) olive oil
1 tablespoon (15 ml) white vinegar
1 tablespoon (15 ml) chopped parsley or cilantro
Salt to taste

Soak the chilies in hot salted water to cover for 30 minutes. Meanwhile, place the onion slices in a bowl with cold salted water to cover for 15 minutes. Drain the onion slices and cook in boiling water to cover for 5 minutes. Drain and set aside. Drain the chilies and purée with the tomatoes in a blender or food mill. In a heavy skillet, heat the lard or oil and fry the tomato-chili mixture over medium heat for about 5 minutes, stirring constantly. Remove from heat and add the onions, olive oil, vinegar, parsley or cilantro and salt to taste.

PURÉ DE PLÁTANO
Banana Purée

This is an unusual sauce for broiled or baked fish, chicken or pork. Use it also as a dessert sauce for fresh fruit or cake.

Makes about 4 cups (1 L)
2 cups (500 ml) hot milk
3 tablespoons (45 ml) sugar
1/2 teaspoon (2 ml) salt
6 ripe large bananas, peeled and mashed
1 tablespoon (15 ml) butter
Grenadine for coloring (optional)

Add the milk, sugar and salt to the mashed bananas. Cook over low heat until thickened, stirring constantly. Add the butter and stir until melted. Add grenadine to make a pale pink sauce.

NUEZ CON MIEL
Walnut and Honey Sauce

Serve over chocolate, coffee or vanilla ice cream, Buñuelos (omit aniseed and syrup) or Plátanos Fritos.

Makes about 1-1/2 cups (375 ml)
1 cup (250 ml) honey
1/2 cup (125 ml) chopped walnuts or chopped
    peeled peanuts

Place the honey in a saucepan and bring to a boil. Boil for 3 minutes, then remove from heat. Let the honey cool slightly, then add the nuts and mix well. Serve warm.

MAIL ORDER SOURCES

Ingredients for Mexican food are becoming more widely available in the United States all the time, and in some parts of the country ingredients such as canned chilies and *masa harina* are routinely available on supermarket shelves. If you are unable to find these or such non-perishable items as corn husks, dried chilies and tortilla presses or other Mexican cooking utensils, check the following mail order sources.

Cal-Foods
195 South 28th Street
San Jose, California 95116
(408) 292-4256
Prices on request. No minimum order.

Casa Gardenas
1758 W. 18th Street
Chicago, Illinois 60607
(312) 733-2891
Prices on request. $15 minimum order.

Casa Moneo
210 West 14th Street
New York, New York 10014
(212) 929-1644
Catalog, $1.50. $15 minimum order, with a $1.00 refund if you have purchased the catalog.

Frank Pizzini
202 Produce Row
San Antonio, Texas 78207
(512) CA7-2082
Prices on request. No minimum order.

Garcia Superette
367 Centre Avenue
Jamaica Plain
Boston, Massachusetts 02130
(617) 524-1521
Price list available. No minimum order.

La Palma Market
2884 24th Street
San Francisco, California 94110
(415) MI8-5500
Prices on request. $5.00 minimum order.

Villareal Market
728 East Haley Street
Santa Barbara, California 93101
(805) 963-2613
Prices on request. No minimum order.

INDEX